Temples along the Nile

Temples Along the Nile

Sarah Symons

Matador
9 Priory Business Park,
Wistow Road, Kibworth Beauchamp,
Leicestershire. LE8 0RX
Tel: 0116 279 2299
Email: books@troubador.co.uk
Web: www.troubador.co.uk/matador
Twitter: @matadorbooks

ISBN 978 1785891 403

British Library Cataloguing in Publication Data.
A catalogue record for this book is available from the British Library.

Printed and bound in the UK by TJ International, Padstow, Cornwall
Typeset in 12pt Bembo by Troubador Publishing Ltd, Leicester, UK

Matador is an imprint of Troubador Publishing Ltd

*In remembrance of my dear sister Ann Ivetta Watson
with whom I shared many happy memories of Egypt.*

And

Mum and Dad who heard it all.

CONTENTS

INTRODUCTION

Following the discovery of Tutankhamun's tomb in 1922, Egypt received world recognition as a cultural treasure house and thousands flocked to The Valley of the Kings to see the treasures of the discovered tombs. It also opened up the Nile as a means of seeing its ancient temples along its banks.

Cruising down the Nile from Luxor to Aswan has long been a popular venture for those of us wishing to see the greatness of those temples along its banks, and even the experience of being on the river has inspired many to seek its pleasures. Certainly to cruise along the best-known river in the world and the longest at 4,160 miles is an experience to be cherished.

In fact, this great river is split into two: the Blue Nile rising in Lake Tana in the Ethiopian mountains, and the White Nile rising in Lake Victoria on the borders of Uganda, them both meeting at Khartoum in the Sudan. Then, as one united river, it travels through the centre of Egypt before discharging into the Mediterranean Sea at the northernmost tip of the country.

This powerful river has, since the beginning of time, given life to the land following its yearly flooding at the end of each May, when rich deposits of black silt brought down from the mountains have nourished the soil to sustain its people with an abundance of crops throughout the ages. This rich deposit of silt gave ancient Egypt the name of "Kemet", the Black Land, and it is known that farming communities have flourished alongside the Nile for six thousand years. Herodotus, the Greek historian (484-425 BC) said that "Egypt was the gift of the Nile", but ancient Egyptians believed that their river was a gift from the gods.

Nowhere on earth has a river like the Nile played such an important role in preserving the life of an entire nation. Without it, the people could not have been fed on such a dry and barren land. Its waters, also the country's main artery, have enabled modern tourism to flourish allowing the visitor to travel by boat to witness the greatness of the Aswan Dam and the temples of Abu Simbel beyond, not to mention seeing memorable vistas along the way. The river has also united the country, providing a valuable route along which commence can travel from one end to the other. It has been said that without the Nile, Egypt could not exist. It brought life to a barren landscape.

The ancient Egyptians believed that the Nile rose out of a cavern fed by a subterranean sea and that the island appearing above the waters was the first land on earth. The ancient Egyptians also believed that all parts of the universe were divine beings and that gods had created them, therefore there was a god or goddess for all aspects of life, with one creator god, Amun, who was depicted with a ram's head. By the time of the New Kingdom (1550-1969 BC), Amun was worshipped throughout Egypt and merged with the god Ra from Heliopolis to become Amun-Ra the supreme god. Even the pharaohs considered him to be their father and dedicated great monuments to him. Great temples, dedicated to other gods and goddesses were built along the banks of the Nile and, having survived the ravages of time, they have provided untold pleasure to thousands of us who have had the good fortune to visit them. In fact the concentration of temples along this stretch of river from Luxor to Aswan has been recognised for being the largest open-air museum in the world.

To visit these magnificent structures was a privilege and a delight, for not only did they stir the imagination they were also a wonderful way of learning about Egypt's historic past. They also enabled us to witness the great artistry of the sculptures and carvings that adorned them, and it was through these carvings that we became acquainted with the ancient gods and goddesses. They became our daily companions as we travelled from one temple to another and provided an everlasting memory of such an enjoyable venture.

MAP OF EGYPT

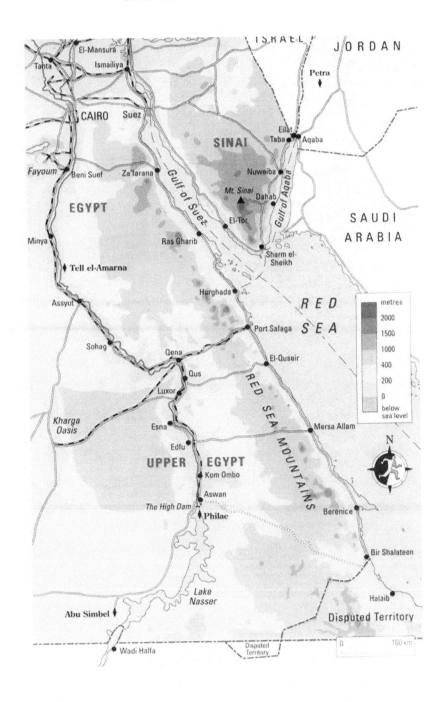

ARRIVAL IN LUXOR

After a five-hour flight from London, the first sight of our destination was the golden sands of the Western Desert. Then the modern buildings of Luxor Airport, which had been built on the edge of the desert, lay beneath the right wing as the aircraft glided in to land. The multitude of palm trees were certainly an indication that we had arrived in Egypt as indeed was the bluest of skies and the bright sunshine. And even though it was late afternoon, we could still feel the heat of the April sun as we were escorted towards Arrivals by white robed personnel.

But arriving in Luxor during the late afternoon was not the best of times when the main road into the centre was packed with a continuous stream of traffic as workers hurried to get home. It was amazing to see how vehicles of all descriptions and state of repair jostled for position with horse-drawn carts and vans packed to capacity with those hitching a lift home, and all oblivious of the dangers of colliding into one another.

Having managed to untangle ourselves from the melee, the coach brought us safely into the centre of Luxor with its fashionable hotels and colourful bazaars. We had reached a more orderly state of things as we drove down its smart corniche – a broad promenade alongside the river – where we were rewarded with a breathtaking view of the river itself, still bustling with passing feluccas and looking very blue. To our left were Luxor's more prestigious landmarks such as the tall colonnades of its temples, followed by the very modern Museum and the Old Winter Palace, whose staircase curved upwards towards its entrance. The well laid out shrubs and places to sit along the corniche gave a good impression of the resort and finally led us to where our Nile cruiser *The Nile Commodore* was moored.

Our baggage had preceded us and was waiting outside our cabins to which we were escorted with great courtesy by stewards in white baggy trousers, red jackets with gold braid and hats to match.

There was a welcoming reception in the salon after an appetising dinner, at which we were able to make friends with our table companions, and since the evening meal had set the standard we would come to expect on our seven day cruise, we excitedly anticipated what had been planned for us. In this respect, we were to be divided into three sizeable groups of around thirty for our excursions with a guide who was expert in Egyptology, and when it was announced that our first venture was to the popular West Bank, the morning could not come quickly enough.

THE WEST BANK: KOM EL HEITAN

COLOSSI OF MEMNON

Our early morning call summoned us to breakfast in time for an eight o'clock departure before the sun became too hot, which was a wise decision as we were soon to discover. We scampered up the steep slope to where our three air-conditioned coaches were parked, and once we had boarded, our respective guides greeted us in Egyptian so we could respond in a similar manner whenever we met. And in this spirit of cordiality and eager anticipation, we crossed the river to the West Bank, and found ourselves travelling through its sun-soaked terrain green with crops that were being irrigated by a network of canals.

With the river behind us, we made for the Theban hills which looked incredibly close in the clear morning air, and in the middle of the broad plain at Kom-el-Heitan, we made a surprising stop to see the iconic Colossi of Memnon.

These amazing statues dominated the entire area, and standing 23m (75ft) high and 20ft across at the shoulders, they dwarfed everyone standing beside them. Although called Memnon, the two statues were really those of the seated pharaoh Amenhotep III (1387-1350 BC) who was also known as Amenophis, the ninth ruler of the 18th Dynasty. He was one of Egypt's greatest rulers, and under his thirty-eight year-old rule, Egypt prospered well, and he also sustained good relations with his neighbours which he encouraged by marrying their princesses. He even married one of his four daughters, princess Sitamun, who then became one of his queens.

The Colossi of Memnon

During his reign, Amenhotep embarked upon an ambitious building programme and was responsible for many of the great monuments we see throughout Egypt, including the great Temple of Amun at Karnak. He filled them with works of art never before seen in the country, having commissioned the best known artists in that period.

His mortuary temple here on the plain at Kom el-Heitan was just as spectacular, and for which these two great figures were created. The temple was also dedicated to Amun, the creator god who was worshipped at Thebes, (now Luxor), and then throughout Egypt. At the time, the temple was the largest that had been built, measuring 700m x 500m/180,000ft and covered a staggering 395,000sq.m/4,200,000sq.ft. The temple was intentionally located in the middle of the plain so that its innermost sanctuary would be flooded during the annual rise of the Nile. This ensured that when the temple reappeared after the river had receded, it would symbolise order and rebirth. A nineteenth-century artist produced a painting showing the flood waters surrounding the Colossi, indicating the vast area the floods covered.

The Colossi, which are among the largest pieces of sculpture ever produced in ancient Egypt, were carved out of a single block of quartzite from the quarries located outside Cairo, 420 miles away. The blocks were brought down the Nile by boat, and weighed a thousand tons each. The statues were put to face east towards the rising sun, and sat outside the first pylon at the temple's entrance. Both statues had suffered the ravages of time, particularly the faces which had almost withered away, but the figures of Amenhotep's mother, Mutemwia, and that of his queen Tiye, standing on either side of the throne, had survived, as had the carved reliefs around the thrones showing the Nile god Hapi entwining plants of lower and upper Egypt in a gesture of unifying the two regions.

The Collossi were called Memnon by early Greek travellers as they thought that the singing noise made by one of the statues at dawn – after it had been severely damaged during the earthquake of 27 BC – was their mythological hero Memnon greeting his mother Eos the Dawn. In fact the sound was said to have been the wind blowing in through one of its cracks. But like the ancient Egyptians, the ancient Greeks also believed deeply in their mythology, and therefore flocked to the damaged statue just to hear their hero 'sing' each dawn. Many slept at the foot of the statue, as to hear his voice was thought to bring them good luck. Among the pilgrims was the Roman Emperor Hadrian who was said to have camped there for several nights. However, after Emperor Septimus Severus had crudely repaired the statue with blocks of matching sandstone in AD 199, the statue 'sang' no more, but as the unique sound had inspired pilgrims for over four hundred years, everyone had become accustomed to calling it Memnon, and the name stuck.

Amenhotep was regarded as a god, as all ancient Egyptians believed that their kings were divine beings chosen by the gods, and that each one had been entered by the spirit of the falcon-god Horus, son of Osiris and Isis, and was therefore the link between them and their gods. At the back of one statue, the words "ruler of rulers" had been carved to describe the pharaoh, but Amenhotep, known as the "Dazzling Sun", styled himself "the dazzling sun disc of the two lands".

Apart from the great Ramses II, there were more statues erected of Amenhotep than any other pharaoh, and this was illustrated here at his mortuary temple where, besides the two enormous statues in front of the entrance pylon, there were two more in front of the second pylon, and a third pair in alabaster standing in front of a third pylon. A long avenue of sphinxes then led from the third pylon westwards to a large solar courtyard containing many more statues of the pharaoh. Also, in the northern half of the temple, there were others carved out of quartzite whilst those in the southern half had been carved in red granite, many of which stood at least 8m (26ft) high. Statues of the goddess Sekhmet were also included. As the daughter of Amun-Ra, she was very much venerated, and many Egyptian pharaohs adopted her to bring them success in battle. She was often depicted with the head of a lioness. Of Sekhmet's statues alone, Amenhotep had included one of her seated and one standing for every day of the year.

Amenhotep described his temple as being "a fortress of eternity for his father, Amun, lord of the two lands". He also described it as "being made of white sandstone, and worked with gold throughout, with its floors purified with silver", and that "its doorways were made of electrum". This latter material was popular in ancient times and was a combination of silver and gold, and had also been used by Hatshepsut to cover her obelisks at Karnak.

As time went by, Amenhotep's great temple began to deteriorate after it had been severely damaged by an earthquake at the time of Merenptah, the thirteenth son of Ramses II who ruled Egypt from 1291-1193 BC, after which, its foundations, weakened by the floods, had become too weak to take the weight of its columns. Consequently, after its walls had collapsed, the temple had become nothing more than a convenient place for obtaining building material, and was stripped of all its precious metals. During Ptolemaic times, the entire compound was said to have been completely covered by a dense grove of acacia trees. From appearances, it looked as if nothing of the temple had survived except for some foundation walls lying alongside the Colossi, but since 2005, archaeologists have excavated along its great length and unearthed one of the pharaoh's statues which they re-erected where it was discovered, and could be seen from the road on a visit in 2010. The excavations were still in progress.

Amenhotep III, "Egypt's dazzling sun" was buried to the west of The Valley of the Kings, known as the West Valley, and was interred in the tomb known as WW22. After mummification, his body was placed inside a nest of gilded and inlaid coffins before being enclosed in a cartouche-shaped red granite sarcophagus. His mummy had, though, been taken from his tomb for safety by local priests who had been worried about the constant plundering in the Valley, and was found by the French explorer, Victor Loret, in 1898, lying among other royal mummies in the tomb of Amenhotep II (numbered KV35), where they had all been stored for safety.

The Colossi have become extremely popular, and tours to the Valley of the Kings often start with a visit here.

The Colossus of Amenhotep III

Mortuary Temple of Amenhotep III
Excavations at Amenhotep's temple with recently discovered statue

THE WEST BANK: DEIR EL-BAHRI

THE MORTUARY TEMPLE OF HATSHEPSUT

Deir el-Bahri was the chosen site of 18th Dynasty Pharaoh Hatshepsut (1479-1458 BC) for her funerary temple, and there, in the great expanse of the valley, we gazed with awe at the splendour of the colonnaded terraces that made up its magnificent structure. Known as Djeser Djeseru (holy of holies), Hatshepsut's "Mansion of a Million Years", as such temples were called, had been built at the foot of the great cliffs which provided a dramatic backcloth to the whole spectacle. And whilst most Theban temples had been built with mud brick walls faced with stone during the 18th Dynasty, Hatshepsut's temple had been built entirely of limestone, causing it to blend in naturally with its surroundings.

The architect of this remarkable structure was Senenmut, who was also Hatshepsut's Chief Steward. He built the temple so that it would be in direct line with Hatshepsut's temple a few miles away across the river at Karnak, an engineering feat he was able to accomplish as, according to modern architects, he was only two degrees out. Senenmut certainly designed the temple on a grand scale by creating an avenue of sphinxes with Hatshepsut's face that rivalled the famous avenue at Karnak, and included flower beds and myrrh trees, all of which have long disappeared. He also placed a pair of stone lions (also missing) at the foot and the bottom of a 30m (100ft) wide ramp or causeway that connected the three great terraces, and completed his design with inspiring rows of colonnades which were considered to be among the greatest pieces of ancient Egyptian art, therefore design of this building an icon of its time, three and a half thousand years ago. It was said that he completed the temple within fifteen years.

Hatshepsut was the eldest daughter of Tuthmosis I, but her royal lineage came from her grandfather, Ahmose who founded the 18th Dynasty in 1525 BC and was the father of Amenhotep I. But, as Amenhotep had died without leaving a male heir, Tuthmosis, a general who had married a royal princess, became Tuthmosis I in 1504 BC. Hatshepsut was married to her half brother who became Tuthmosis II, but when he died, his son by a minor wife succeeded him, and being too young, Hatshepsut became co-regent and later, as was her birthright, she assumed full powers as Pharaoh in 1479 BC and ruled Egypt for the next twenty-one years, during which,

Hatshepsut's Mortuary Temple

she brought peace and prosperity to the country, and was regarded as one of Egypt's greatest monarchs.

Since it was unknown for a woman to become pharaoh, Hatshepsut made herself more acceptable and conformed to tradition by assuming the outward appearance of a man. She also walked like a man and was depicted wearing a false beard.

According to mythology, she was fathered by Amun-Ra, who disguised himself as Tuthmosis I and entered the bed-chamber of his queen Ahmose-Nefertari who then gave birth to Hatshepsut. The story goes that Amun-Ra also sought the help of Khnum, the god creator who fashioned people on his potters wheel, and who breathed life into Hatshepsut's figure saying she would be "supreme among men, as has been commanded by your father" (Amun-Ra). The god then presented his daughter to all the assembled gods and gave her the kiss of power. Hatshepsut's divine conception and birth featured in many of the temple's reliefs, with one showing her kneeling before Amun-Ra and his consort Amunet.

Deir el Bahri, whose name means "Monastery of the North" was once inhabited by the early Christians who turned Hatshepsut's temple into a monastery and contributed to the defacing of many of the temple's carvings believing them to be pagan. But it was Hatshepsut's jealous successor, Tuthmosis III, who really set about destroying all evidence of his stepmother, by defacing her images and scratching out her cartouches. He even squared the rounded columns of the lower terrace in order to remove all references of her and those of his grandfather, Tuthmosis I. But despite this destruction, it is fortunate that evidence remained to record her important role in Egyptian history. Another pharaoh, Akenhaten, also vented his wroth on the temple by removing all images of Amun when he abandoned him and other deities to worship the sun god Aken and established a new religion in Egypt. He even incorporated the god's name into his own.

Exploring Hatshepsut's mortuary temple was an experience that would be long remembered. As each of the three terraces and their colonnades were approached by the two long ramps with a central staircase, it made reaching them far easier than expected with a glorious view at the top.

The first significant feature close to the entrance of the first terrace was Senenmut's burial chamber. Inside, the tomb contained a portrait of the architect with decorations of the constellations and months of the year spread across the ceiling. For some reason, the tomb was never completed.

Neither did it contain his body. It was taken across to the necropolis of Shiek Abat at Quarna to be buried there.

The first ramp which divided the first colonnade, took us above and over it to the enormous space that was the second terrace with its own ramp leading to another double row of elegant columns at the far end. There, the columns contained the best preserved reliefs of Hatshepsut's divine conception and birth, and the whole of the portico was decorated with ritual scenes of hunting and fishing, and included scenes of the erection of the two obelisks she had installed in front of her father's temple at Karnak, and which provided more vital information about her reign. To the right of the colonnade was a chapel dedicated to Anubis, the black-headed god of mummification and the dead, and contained reliefs of Hatshepsut and Tuthmosis III as co-rulers in the presence of three gods: Anubis, Re-Horakhty, another name for Horus and shown as a falcon-headed man but with a sun disc above his head, and the goddess Hathor with cow-like ears, but the images of Hatshepsut had been defaced. Fortunately, the colours of the chapel had been perfectly preserved and were a joy to see. However, one scene showing Hatshepsut worshipping Hathor had escaped damage, as it had been too high for the vandals to reach. To the left of the colonnade was the chapel dedicated to Hathor, in which the top of each of the twelve columns was decorated with the goddess's face, as at her temple at Dendara.

But the most outstanding feature of the temple were the colossal figures of Hatshepsut standing against the columns of the third terrace in the traditional pose of Osiris, wearing the double crown of Egypt and holding the insignia of office – the crook and flail with crossed arms. These Osiride statues showed her with a beard, and it was just possible to make out the cord attaching it to her face. One of her limestone heads, with the face showing much of its original colouring had been taken away to the Cairo Museum.

Beyond the third terrace, the upper most part of the temple also contained a Sanctuary to Amun which was entered through a pink granite doorway that led directly into the cliff. A tomb had also been prepared for Hatshepsut, but that too had not contained her body.

After Hatshepsut's death in 1458 BC, the temple became a place for pilgrimage and the scene of great processions during the *Beautiful Feast of the Valley* which took place every year. But later, the temple was reduced to ruin by her successor Tuthmosis III who went on a malicious rampage of destroying as much as he could.

Since its first discovery in 1881 when the temple was engulfed in sand, various explorations have been carried out, the most notable by the Metropolitan Museum of Art in 1934, when the full scale of the destruction came to light with smashed statues and sphinxes lying in a pit in front of the temple. The Museum set about repairing the Osiride statues and other features, and in recent times, a Polish archaeological team arrived in 1961, and were successful in restoring the third terrace back to its former beauty.

The whereabouts of Hatshepsut's missing mummy had been a mystery ever since the royal tombs were first discovered. She was known to have favoured burial deep inside the cliffs, as it was thought to have been a far safer option than other methods of burial in pyramidal structures. Consequently, a well hidden cliff tomb had been prepared for her in the Valley of the Kings (KV 20), and when Howard Carter discovered it some 70m (230ft) above ground level in 1903, he found it had been plundered of all its valuable items.

When he had entered the burial chamber via a long sloping corridor, he found two sarcophagi, but it was the large yellow quartzite one with the figure of Isis at its foot that attracted his attention. The lid, which had been dislodged, was inscribed "great royal wife and lady of the two lands, Hatshepsut", confirming at last that this was Hatshepsut's burial place, and he had found her sarcophagus. But it was empty. Both her coffin and body were missing. To Carter's surprise, the other sarcophagus was inscribed with the name of Tuthmosis I, implying that Hatshepsut had intended the tomb to be the burial place for herself and her father, but Tuthmosis' coffin and body were also missing. Actually, they had been removed by Tuthmosis III for burial in the Valley of the Kings (KV38), and this tomb was eventually discovered by the French explorer, Victor Loret, in 1899.

Apart from the sarcophagi, the only visible finds in KV20 were broken pieces of pottery, jars and some limestone blocks. However, as the walls of the tomb had been unsuitable for decoration, the artists had used these blocks to inscribe funerary texts in black and red, and fifteen of them had been illustrated with stick-like figures and scenes from the *Amduat* - a book of the Underworld buried with the dead.

The builder of this particular tomb had been Ireni, architect to Tuthmosis I, and Howard Carter noted that even though the corridors twisted and turned for more than 214m (699ft) beyond the entrance, they had been specially enlarged to allow Hatshepsut's enormous sarcophagus to glide safely down to its final resting place. A feat indeed, since the burial chamber was located 97m (318ft) below the surface. Howard Carter later made the comment that this particular tomb which was the deepest in the Valley and considered to have been the most dangerous to enter, "had been one of the most irksome pieces of work" he had undertaken.

Meanwhile, the search for Hatshepsut's body continued throughout the twentieth century, but as the priests of the 21ˢᵗ Dynasty had obviously moved her body along with other pharaohs to places of safety, it was difficult to find. However, items bearing her name appeared in two separate tombs. The first was a wooden box inscribed with her cartouche and containing her mummified liver or spleen, found inside a deep cliff tomb at Deir el-Bahri in 1881, and the other was her beautifully painted coffin found by John Romer, an archaeologist, in 1961, whilst he was clearing out the shaft of Ramses XI's tomb (KV4). How it got there remained a mystery, but it might have been the act of a well meaning priest.

However, the saga regarding the whereabouts of Hatshepsut's mummy continued, starting when decades before, whilst Howard Carter was excavating in the Valley of the Kings, he came across the tomb numbered KV60 whose corridor had cut into a neighbouring tomb (KV19). Inside, he found two female mummies, one inside a coffin and the other lying unwrapped on the floor. He also found some mummified geese. The mummy lying on the floor had been laid out in the pose of a queen and, according to her size and well worn teeth, Carter described her as "a mature and obese woman". There is no record of any action taken by him, only that he took the geese and left the mummies where he had found them before closing up the tomb. Three years later, another archaeologist visited the tomb and took away the mummy inside the coffin which, according to an inscription, was identified as Hatshepsut's wet nurse. Thereafter, the single occupant of KV60 lay forgotten as the tomb disappeared into obscurity when its entrance could not be found. But in 1978, Donald Ryan, an American Egyptologist and lecturer, decided to investigate the mysterious "mature lady" and sought out the lost tomb. He eventually found it after sweeping away the debris of KV19 that had been obstructing it. Upon entering, he found the burial chamber in much the same condition as when Carter had left it, but concerned to see the elderly mummy lying in such an undignified manner on the floor, he and his companion ordered a coffin to be made in which they then placed her for transference to Cairo. There was no hint that this might have been the body of Hatshepsut until 2006, when Dr. Zahi Hawass, the eminent Egyptian archaeologist and head of Egyptian Antiquities in Cairo, ordered that all the 18th Dynasty mummies in the Cairo Museum, including the unknown lady, be X-rayed to solve the mystery once and for all. He even ordered an X-ray of Hatshepsut's wooden box, containing her mummified organs, and when this was scanned, the box also contained a single tooth. This curious discovery then led to all the mummies' jaws being re-X-rayed, and the marvellous outcome was that the tooth fitted the empty space in the unknown mummy's upper right jaw, proving beyond doubt that the long neglected lady was "her majesty king Hatshepsut herself". It is probable that the tooth had loosened during mummification and that an observant embalmer had saved it for posterity. A C.T. scan revealed that Hatshepsut had probably died of an infection following an abscessed tooth turning cancerous, which would have caused her last days to end in considerable pain. But with so much interest in modern times focused on Egypt's rich and often romantic past, it was fitting that modern technology had finally identified the body of one of Egypt's greatest pharaohs, thus enabling her to take her rightful place alongside her father and other royal kinfolk in the Cairo Museum.

THE MORTUARY TEMPLE OF MENTUHOTEP II

To the left of Hatshepsut's Mortuary Temple lay the ones of Mentuhotep II, founder of the 11th Dynasty (2040 BC), and was the oldest temple yet discovered. It appeared to have had some of its lower terrace still in place with stubs of its once elegant pillars standing about a metre high, but the entire area was littered with blocks of fallen masonry and assorted rubble.

The temple was considered to have been the earliest of the royal cult complexes of the Middle Kingdom, as during the 11th Dynasty, the rulers of Thebes built their tombs at El Tarif on the northern end of the Theban necropolis, and were constructed as over-sized private tombs, but Mentuhotep's temple which was also his burial place, had been built on a high platform and set into the cliffs with a large court complex with terraces and ramps. It was thought that Senenmut had copied these features into Hatshepsut's temple. But the most notable feature of Mentuhotep's temple had been the enormous pyramid that had once surmounted the colonnaded structure on the second terrace. It had been destroyed with the rest of the structure.

An earlier excavation of this temple uncovered the entrance to the tomb passage and a large hall with eighty-two octagonal pillars which was thought to have been where offerings to the dead pharaoh and gods had been made.

A surprising incident occurred there during Howard Carter's visit in 1900, when the horse he was riding loosened the ground beneath its feet and revealed an underground chamber in which the seated figure of Mentuhotep was brought to light. This miraculous discovery enabled yet another precious example of ancient sculpture to be salvaged and added to the long list of ancient treasures to be seen at the Cairo Museum.

THE MORTUARY TEMPLE OF TUTHMOSIS III

This mortuary temple was less recognisable and lay in total ruin upon the landscape. It had not been as large as its neighbour and had apparently been stripped of its stonework during the progressive building programme of the Rameside period.

It was time to depart, and as we took one last glimpse of Hatshepsut's Mansion of a Million Years, we felt privileged that we had witnessed its beauty which had been brought about by the expertise of modern archaeologists, enabling it to grace the landscape for maybe another thousand years.

Trays of refreshing orange and lemonade along with blissful cooling shade welcomed us back on board *The Nile Commodore*, as did the prospect of a good meal after such an eventful morning. And once on board, we soon found ourselves gliding across calm waters with a refreshing breeze that enticed many of us after lunch to head for the top deck. There, we could either relax with a book beneath the protective awning that stretched across its central sitting area, or have a dip in the stern's bathing pool. Either way, the sun deck was the best place to be with the river banks providing a never ending picture of everyday life that was filled with variety and colour. Our presence on the river also generated a great deal of interest from the shore as groups of excited children ran alongside and waved frantically at us; their smiles broadening into large grins as we waved back.

Then, at four o'clock precisely, a bell summoned everyone for afternoon tea on the deck. It was also a good time when everyone could come together and mull over the morning's events and, as the days went by, it proved to be a very popular event.

THE WEST BANK: DEIR EL BAHRI

THE RAMESSEUM:
MORTUARY TEMPLE OF RAMSES II

Whilst on the West Bank, there was one other iconic building that warranted a visit, and that was Ramses II's Mortuary Temple which had partly survived since its construction in the fourteenth century BC. The temple was also known as the Ramesseum, a name given to it in modern times by the French scholar, Jean Champillion, who had deciphered Ramses' throne name of *Userma-maat-re-setep-en-ra* from a cartouche found on the site. It meant "Keeper of Harmony and Balance, Strong in Right, and Elect of Ra". Champillion was also the first man to have mastered the meaning of the Egyptian hieroglyphic writing system in 1822, after studying it with two other ancient writings inscribed on the Rosetta Stone, now in the British Museum.

Built by the great pharaoh himself, the temple stood in solitary isolation on the desert plain, on the edge of the Theban necropolis, a short distance from the Valley of the Kings and, along with Hatshepsut's Mortuary Temple, it was regarded as one of the grandest buildings along the West Bank. It is possible that Ramses had chosen this site because it was where his father, Seti I, had built one before it collapsed.

At first sight, there were no signs of an outside wall or roof. Only the surviving columns outlined its grandeur. And whilst the temple had been robbed of its stone and much of its statuary had disappeared, it still revealed itself to be a dominant structure on the deserted landscape. Ramses had built the temple soon after his coronation in 1304 BC when he was twenty-five years of age, and it took twenty years in the making. During his sixty-seven year reign Ramses embellished it with colossal statues of himself and carved inscriptions showing himself in the presence of gods and defeating his Hittite enemies at Kadash (now Syria), in order to immortalise himself, not only as a great monarch, but as a successful warrior. But, Ramses never defeated the Hittite army. It was true that he headed his troops out to meet them in battle, but when he got to the scene he was tricked into believing they were elsewhere and he found himself trapped. Ramses luckily escaped, and he eventually made peace with the Hittite King many years later by signing the first ever treaty made and by marrying the king's daughter.

The Ramesseum

Like Hatshepsut's Mortuary Temple, the Ramesseum was also called "Mansion of a Million Years", but it differed in design, having only one storey with a long rectangular shape. It also exceeded the grandeur of Amenhotep III's temple. The complex surrounding the Ramesseum originally covered fifteen acres and included a separate palace for Ramses and his family; a temple dedicated to his mother, Queen Tuya; a Mammisi (the first of its kind where the birth of a young god was celebrated), and a Sacred Lake where priests bathed to purify themselves each morning before performing their daily rituals of offering gifts to the gods. The complex also had servants quarters, magazines on either side of the temple for storing food, and barns for the herds of goats and sheep that supplied the temple with fresh meat and milk. But all of the above mentioned buildings had disappeared except for the magazines on the north-eastern side of the temple.

There had also been a monumental gate at the entrance of the complex, and a small landing stage for barges on the banks of the Nile, but these had also disappeared, as had the Nile, which had changed its course further to the south.

The present entry into the temple complex was through the Second Courtyard which faced the temple, and it was here that the great space of the complex was most noticeable. Behind, lay the great expanse of the First Forecourt which still had its two traditionally shaped pylons still standing to mark the southern end of the complex. Each pylon measured 60m across, but only one side was visible facing inwards. The other side had been blocked off for safety purposes as an overgrown thicket had grown right up against the pylon. The inside walls glorified Ramses' victories over his enemies with the vanquished lying at his feet, but as the stonework was in such a poor condition with the stone blocks looking as though they were about to fall down, it made the scenes disjointed, and it was not possible to fully appreciate the lively carvings. Behind the pylons there had once been a perimeter road that had surrounded the entire complex and given access to the Nile where the barges had once moored.

The first great forecourt had been swept clear of all broken masonry, and at one time there had been an enormous quartzite statue of Ramses dominating the top right hand corner. As it was estimated to have been about 20m (56ft) high, it had rivalled the Colossi of Memnon, and would certainly have presented an awesome spectacle to those entering the temple in Ramses' time. In fact, early Greek travellers had equalled it to Amenhotep's statues and had called it "the young Memnon". Unfortunately, it had fallen victim to an earthquake around the end of the first century AD and had collapsed in pieces, severing the head which had crashed into the second courtyard. It was also estimated to have weighed around 1,000 tons. However, when the Italian explorer, Giovani Belzoni, visited the site in 1816, under the patronage of Sir Henry Salt, the British Consul in Cairo, he removed the head for transportation back to Cairo. But as the 3m (9ft) tall head weighed 7 tons, he had to have a team of local men to drag it across the desert to the waiting boat. Salt then presented the head to the British Museum in 1818 where it has been on display ever since. Ramses had the head carved in a much lighter stone to the rest of the statue in order to make it more noticeable, and this had certainly been the case, as the yellow coloured bust has been the Egyptian Hall's main attraction ever since.

The Portico

The fallen Colossus of Ramses lying at the top end of the Second Court

The second forecourt with its original paving still intact had also been swept clear. It too had once been flanked by colonnades, but a solitary ruin situated midway between the second pylons and the main temple revealed a very decorative portico with four Osiride statues of Ramses holding the crook and flail of kingship. This building had been left neglected and was surrounded by shrubbery with a tree growing out of its interior, but inside it was an archaeological gem. Along with the four statues, the walls were covered with hieroglyphs and very attractive carvings. To what building the portico had belonged there was no way of knowing, but as Ramses was portrayed in such a kingly manner, it would have played an important role in the life of the complex. At the top right hand corner of the second forecourt, were large fragments of another colossus of Ramses, lying face downwards where it had fallen, probably as a result of the same earthquake. Judging from the size of an isolated foot, and the size of the head which showed Ramses wearing the distinctive striped *Nemes* headdress, it too had matched the size of the other statue. There was a cartouche stamped on his left shoulder. The haphazardness of broken masonry was a reminder as to how the area must have looked when the first archaeologists visited the site in the nineteenth century. The second forecourt had also included some more colossi of Ramses, two of which had shown him seated at the bottom of the steps leading into the main temple and wearing the domed-shaped double crown of Egypt. However, only the black granite head of the right hand side one had survived and had been mounted on a concrete plinth to prevent it from being taken away. Although the double crown had a slice taken out of it, and Ramses' nose had been damaged, it did not in any way detract from the beauty of the sculpture nor the fine features showing Ramses with a wisp of a smile. It was a remarkable portrait of the king. Standing over 3m high, the head dwarfed anybody standing next to it. The seated colossus on the opposite side had almost disappeared. Only the base and the lower legs of the colossus had survived. It was probable that the rest of the remaining statue had been taken away to some museum.

Down the western side of the first forecourt there had been a double row of columns which had fronted the Royal Palace where Ramses and his family had stayed to participate in the celebrations of *The Feast of the Beautiful Valley* held every second month of the summer. When the royal residence was excavated in 2009, it revealed it to have numerous rooms which had been separated by partition walls. These partitions had been heightened to about one metre, in order to give visitors a better view of the palace's layout. In the centre was one enormous room which had probably been used on ceremonial occasions when Ramses entertained his visiting dignitaries.

Beyond the palace lay the domestic quarters and kitchens which had also been excavated at the same time, and as they had been sited close to the magazines on that side of the temple, they had been conveniently placed for cooks to receive their daily supply of food. The excavations unearthed one kitchen with three wells in its floor, whilst another still had its oven in the top right corner. Standing about a metre high, the little oven had a flat top on which the bread was baked, and a space underneath for lighting the fire. The discovery of first century pottery there indicated that these rooms had been inhabited during the Roman period. However a pile of broken cups and plates found there had been swept aside into one corner.

But the main attraction of the entire temple complex was undoubtedly the magnificent looking Portico of the Grand Hypostyle Hall (a roof supported by pillars) which had given such an impressive introduction to the temple upon arriving at the site with its four Osiride figures of Ramses standing against each pillar, arms crossed and holding the crook and flail of kingship. However, all the heads had been destroyed, and one face vandalised. Nevertheless, the entire facade presented a powerful image and gave photographers a brilliant picture with the golden-yellow of the stonework creating a stunning contrast against a bright blue sky.

Once through the portico, the bright sunshine illuminated the interior of the roofless Hypostyle Hall, and made it possible to appreciate the beautiful

The Granite Head

carvings on all of its thirty-nine surviving columns, highlighting important events in Ramses' life, as well as presenting him in the presence of many gods, chiefly Amun, to whom he dedicated the temple. A famous one showed Amun writing Ramses' name on a leaf with Seshat, the goddess of writing – who recorded everything – looking on. Another relief showed Amun attending Ramses' coronation beneath which was a panel showing a procession of twenty-three of Ramses' one hundred and eleven sons. He also had fifty-seven daughters. This example of including his children in his dedications and placing them around his statues presented him as a devoted father.

Originally, the Hall had forty-eight columns to support the roof. The central columns had their capitals in the shape of an open papyrus flower, whilst the others were in the shape of a bud, and all looking as impressive as those in the Hypostyle Hall at Karnak. The columns were covered with lively carvings showing Ramses making offerings to the gods with the falcon god Horus very much in prominence. His was among the most recognisable of the figures. With no forms of lighting in the place, the temple had originally been lit by natural light coming through the clerestory windows set high up in the walls.

Beyond the Hall were two smaller hypostyle halls, the first of which still had its eight columns in place. Called the Astronomical Room, there had once been a twelve-month calendar painted across its ceiling. It was considered to have been the earliest example ever found which reflected the brilliance of the ancient Egyptians in astrology. This room also featured a picturesque relief of priests carrying the sacred boats of Amun, his wife Mut and their son Khonsu. There was another delightful one showing Seshat and Thoth writing Ramses' name on a leaf.

The next hall had some of its columns missing, but the architraves above the existing ones still showed the original artwork of hieroglyphic signs and other symbols painted in red, dark blue and yellow. As the ancient Egyptians loved bright colours, it was possible that the room had also been painted to match the architraves.

Beyond the Hall had been the Sanctuaries where religious ceremonies had been conducted by the priests and where Ramses had communed with his god Amun. But these had also completely disappeared with the area they had occupied completely swept clear of all broken masonry. Only the circular bases of their columns were visible above ground. This clearance had left a large empty void which tended to accentuate the great length of the temple. In this respect it resembled the great expanse of Amenhotep's Mortuary Temple.

The complete disappearance of the Sanctuaries had also left the temple to end rather abruptly with another set of four Osiride statues of Ramses standing against the outside of the last surviving wall of the second Hypostyle Hall. And as they were facing outwards and opposite to those at the entrance, they made an appropriate ending to the existing temple.

However, the surviving remnants of the magazines, made more recognisable by their domed roofs, were accessible at this point, and it was possible to walk into them. They had been extremely important as they had been capable of storing food for as many as 30,000 people; Ramses having ensured that there was enough food for everyone in case the crops failed. It had been documented that the craftsmen living nearby who had built and decorated the tombs, used to stage protests outside the Ramesseum when they did not get their prescribed food rations. And long after Ramses' death when there was no more money left in the temple's coffers, the priests and the servants looking after the temple were given food in lieu of wages. But when both the money and the food ran out the temple was abandoned, thus bringing to an end its long productive life.

During Ramses' lifetime, the Ramesseum had served as a religious centre where daily offerings were made to Amun and other deities. But after Ramses' death in 1213 BC, it remained as a focal point for *The Feast of the Beautiful Valley*. And papyrus found during the reign of Ramses IX, some ninety years after Ramses' death, showed that the temple continued to play an important role in the social life of the community. The continued use of the temple was supervised by the attending priests whose role was to ensure that Ramses' name was kept alive for all eternity. Merneptah too, Ramses' thirteenth son who later became pharaoh, also played his part.

But, after the abandonment of the temple, it and its palaces became the victims of the stone robbers and those who stole its fine furnishings and ripped the electrum off its walls. The Mammisi itself was dismantled by the Ptolemaic monarchs who ruled Egypt from 323 BC – 30 BC when their last queen, Cleopatra died. The monarchs also removed the stonework to build their own temples down the Nile Valley.

The Ramesseum was certainly a lasting memorial to the great Ramses II, and although there was very little left of the interior apart from the very decorative columns, the temple still provided the visitor with a wealth of interest, with the spirit of Ramses dominating every single corner.

The Ramesseum: Cartouche of Ramses II

The Ramesseum: The End Wall with Osiride figures of Ramses

The Domed Store Houses

Hypostyle Hall; Relief of Seated Amun presenting Ramses with the key of life, with Sekhmet and Khonsu, Son of Amun (left) in attendance

THE WEST BANK: MEDINAT HABU

MORTUARY TEMPLE OF RAMSES III

About one and a half miles to the south west of the Ramesseum, and within sight of the Theban hills lay another pharaonic gem at Medinat Habu where Ramses III (1184-1153BC), the first pharaoh of the 20th Dynasty, built his Mortuary Temple. Ramses III modelled his Mansion of a Million Years on the Ramesseum, and when completed, it was second in size only to the great temple at Karnak. It had also been very well preserved. Ramses probably built there as the site was one of the first places in Thebes to be associated with the local god Amun, and it was also the centre of economic life there. The temple had even been large enough to take into protection the entire population of Thebes during the Libyan invasions.

The Temple was situated at the far end of the busy town whose buildings had almost reached its front gate, but visitors were being directed through a purposely built entrance in the south west corner. Once inside, we were confronted by the enormous open space of its forecourt, in which lay the ancient ruins of the Chapels of the Votaresses, built for the high priestesses of Amun, and which had remained the object of veneration long after Ramses' temple had been abandoned.

Medinat Habu Courtyard: Mortuary Temple of Ramses III

Cartouche of Ramses III

Immediately in front and commanding the far end of the forecourt were the towering walls of the First Pylon which gave access into the actual temple, and like his predecessor, Ramses III had also covered them with scenes of his military exploits, an idea he copied from the Ramesseum, showing him overpowering the Nubians and Syrians, although he never went to war with either. But on the inner walls of the pylon there were scenes of his actual exploits with his oversized figure scattering his enemies from his chariot. Additional scenes showed his scribes making a tally of the prisoners by counting their severed hands and genitals in order to assess each soldier's reward in gold. Unlike the walls at the Ramesseum, the First Pylon was in a much better state of preservation, thus making the scenes clearer to see.

The pylon gave way into the First Court which made an elegant entrance to the temple with its flanking columns situated on the right, against which stood the imposing Osiride figures of Ramses III, albeit without their heads. The damage had probably occurred when the Court was occupied by Coptic Christians who lived there right up to the nineteenth century when they were finally removed. Standing beside each figure was a knee-high statue of his queen, but the faces of all except one had withered away. Abutting the Court on the left were the remaining walls of the Royal Palace with its interesting array of hieroglyphs including a large cartouche of its owner. Standing against the walls and facing its twin on the other side, was a statue of Sekhmet. She carried pilgrims' prayers to Amun who "resided" in the temple. And, above us, and spanning our pathway, was a covered bridge which had once led from the palace. In its centre was a rectangular opening called the Window of Appearances from which Ramses presented himself to his people. Decorating the window were reliefs of prisoners' heads for which Ramses also rewarded his military commanders with gold collars.

The Second Pylon lay ahead, and its outside walls displayed more military scenes of Ramses leading six rows of prisoners towards Amun and his vulture goddess wife, Mut. This was accompanied by a long text lauding his victories in Asia Minor. Above, the ceiling of the gateway had been decorated with winged cobras and sun discs which still showed their original colours. Its massive door, however, was still in place and both its sides had once displayed brightly coloured scenes to match the interior. Behind the pylon lay the Second Court, another open square with a single line of columns flanking each side, and a double row at its head. There had also been Osiride figures of Ramses standing beside each one, but during Coptic times they were removed to make way for a church and a thick layer of mud was plastered over the reliefs. These scenes, showing the annual festivals of Min and Sokar, had eventually been restored to show their original colours.

Mortuary Temple of Ramses III
Sekhmet outside Ramses' Palace

The double row of columns at the top of the Court appeared to be a fitting entrance into the Hypostyle Hall with its thicket of twenty-four exotic looking columns covered with images of Ramses interacting with various gods, and all their colours creating a glorious sight. The Hall had also been aptly called the Chamber of Columns, and as each one presented a memorable image, it was not possible to single out any specific favourite. The colourful display continued in the treasure chambers where valuables bestowed upon the temple had been kept. Its columns showed items such as gold, lapis lazuli and myrrh being weighed in glorious detail and colour. This gave a great insight into the many activities carried out at the temple. On the other side were the five Chapels dedicated to Ramses himself, his predecessor, Ramses II, and the gods Osiris, Ptah and Sokar.

Hypostyle Hall: Relief of Seated Amun presenting Ramses (right) with symbol of kingship

Our attention was drawn to the fact that all the reliefs had been deeply incised into the walls to make sure that they could not be used again by successive artists, as sometimes had been the case. This naturally ensured that the legacy of Ramses III would last for ever.

The temple continued with two smaller chambers, one of which was the Funerary Chamber of Ramses III where reliefs showed Thoth writing his name on the sacred tree of Heliopolis.

Then, the temple suddenly opened out into the bright sunshine where some of the columns had only survived to about waist height. They had been decorated with a triangular pattern that had not been seen in any of the other temples, and were an attractive addition to the hieroglyphs which appeared to have a greater definition in the bright sunlight. There too, the outside walls of the last surviving chamber had been decorated with a calendar showing the dates of the various festivals. Storehouses, such as those at the Ramesseum had also surrounded the temple, but these had almost crumbled away.

After retracing our footsteps back to the great open space of the forecourt we passed the little ruined temple that had been partially built by Hatshepsut nearly three hundred years before Ramses III had laid his first stone. She had also decorated its interior, but her cartouches and images had been erased by Tuthmosis III. They were later restored by Horemheb and Seti I. Some of the reliefs there showed Tuthmosis III presiding over its foundations by stretching the measuring tape in the presence of Seshat who was the goddess responsible for measuring and recording all things created.

Interestingly too, a little distance to the left was a Nilometer, which had been connected to the Nile by a canal, and had warned the temple of imminent flooding. There had also been a small Sacred Lake situated almost immediately behind the enclosure wall in the south-east corner.

Exit was through the Syrian Gate, the actual entrance to the temple, and so named after the Syrian fortress whose lofty gatehouse had impressed Ramses. It was in the gatehouse that he had housed his harem and where he had frequently relaxed. Originally, the surrounding area had been a garden and, as there were some palm trees around, it was possible to visualise how the temple must have looked in Ramses' time.

Medinat Habu: Hypostyle Hall

Medinat Habu: The remains of the furthermost point of the Temple

LUXOR

Luxor was a busy and noisy town with taxis and horse-drawn carriages making their way up and down the corniche, but ignoring the bustle, the greatest joy was its magnificent temple, situated in the centre of the town, and whose columns we had seen from the corniche across the road.

The temple fully portrayed the splendour of ancient Thebes which became the capital of Egypt after Montuhotep II of the 11th Dynasty (2055 BC) reunited the country after years of fragmentation. Thebes had been inhabited for at least 6,000 years, and had been visited by the ancient Greeks as early as the eighth century BC when Homer called it an "Egyptian Treasure House" and the 'City of a Hundred Gates'. He even mentioned it in his *Iliad*. Herodotus, the Greek Historian (484-424 BC), also visited and expounded its unique beauty, which was praise indeed since ancient Greece had her own spectacular architecture. Centuries later, the Romans built a military fortress adjacent to the Temple which the Arabs called Al Uqsur, and this is how the town got the name of Luxor.

In the 18th Dynasty, Amenhotep III (1417-1379 BC) included Thebes in his adventurous building programme and dedicated this great temple to his "father Amun" and to Mut and Khonsu, but as he had died before the work was completed, his successor Ramses II continued with the building and added some refinements of his own.

After centuries of neglect, the temple was discovered by the French archaeologist Gaston Maspero in 1881, who found the temple partially buried under mounds of sand and debris that had accumulated over the centuries. Only the tops of columns, obelisks and colossi were visible. They had also been blackened by the domestic fires of the shanty town that had been built on top. Another anomaly was the fact that the fourteenth century Abu Haggag Mosque had been built over its south-west corner, and whilst the offending homesteads had been removed, they could not remove the Mosque. It was considered too important, being the burial place of their patron saint, Abu Haggag, and had been built by their hero Badr al Gamali to celebrate his victories over the Nubians in 1077.

Our introduction to the temple had been the sight of its enormous columns from the corniche across the way, and when we arrived visitors were already milling around the site with dozens of cars and coaches parked in the enormous area leading to its entrance. Immediately we were overawed at the sight of the twin towers of the First Pylon rising 24m (72ft) high and stretching 65m (195ft) across. This had been built by Ramses II who used the walls to publicise his military exploits at the Battle of Qadesh in 1274 BC. He also included the two enormous granite statues of himself seen seated on either side of the entrance. The two thrones had equally been decorated with reliefs, to show the Nile god binding the symbols of the two lands of Egypt together in an act of union. Originally there had been six colossi in front of the pylon, but only the two seated ones and another of Ramses standing on his own had survived. The surviving head from one of the missing statues was lying on its own on the ground, and miraculously it had escaped damage from its fall. This imposing façade had also been endowed with two pink granite obelisks standing 16m (82ft) high and tipped with electrum, but there was only one on site. The other had been given as a gift to the French Government by the ruler of Luxor, Mohammed Ali in 1833 in recognition of Champollion's achievements in deciphering the hieroglyphics. When the artist David Roberts visited the site at the beginning of the excavations in 1885, he recorded the scene on canvas showing that the sand had surrounded the obelisks and had reached the lap of the seated Ramses.

Inspired, we passed through the entrance into the Court of Ramses II also added by Ramses. It consisted of a large open square surrounded on three sides by a double row of columns with papyrus bud capitals, but as the walls of the Mosque had infiltrated into the south west corner of the Court, they had broken the line of columns along that side, and had therefore left a narrower entrance. In between each column there was a tall statue of Ramses, but those at the top end of the Court had been beheaded and some of the columns had been reduced to half their height, otherwise the rest of the colonnade provided an excellent picture as to how grand the Court had once looked. In Ramses' day, the columns had been covered over to form arcades.

The Right hand Row of the Avenue of Sphinx

The only Sphinx whose features have survied undamaged

Ramses II guarding the entrance into the Temple

Earlier, there had been a small shrine that Tuthmosis III had dedicated to Khonsu, but only the four columns and their architraves of its fine portico could be seen. These had also jutted outwards to narrow the entrance leading into the next section of the Temple.

It was on the opposite side at the top right had corner of the Court that Ramses, along with his queen and a retinue of sons had worshipped and offered gifts to Mut and to Mont the Theban war god. There too, the ancient artists had recorded in relief the grand processions which had taken place there each year at the Fesitval of Opet. This was the most holy of all the processions when the image of Amun was brought from Karnak by sacred barge to reside inside the temple. It had started on the nineteenth day of the second month of the flood (late August), and lasted for more than two weeks. There too, flanking the exit were two more colossi of Ramses seated on his throne, but this time in black granite. They made imposing figures and dwarfed everybody passing underneath. Equally interesting were the deeply incised hieroglyphic figures and signs on the side of the thrones with figures of bound prisoners from Nubia and Asia around the bases; again Ramses had taken the opportunity of publicising his military exploits.

These magnificent figures led into the Colonnade of Amenhotep III which comprised of a double row of columns, stretching 52m (162ft) in a long spectacular and elegant avenue. Again the columns were topped with distinctive papyrus bud capitals. It was these lofty columns we had seen from the roadside with their massive architraves balancing precariously above them. Tutankhamun had also made his contribution to the temple by decorating the walls behind the columns with more scenes of the Opet Festival showing acrobats, musicians and dancers joining in the processions. On the western wall was an image of Tutankhamun himself, but the cartouches belonged to his successor, Horemheb.

At the top end of the Colonnade lay the Court of Amenhotep III, another large open square surrounded on all three sides by another double row of columns which were the best preserved in the entire temple. In 1989, restoration work was carried out on the Colonnade as it was feared that the constant flooding had undermined its foundations, and during the excavation work, twenty-two statues from the New Kingdom were miraculously found and taken to the Luxor Museum. Then, after securing the foundations, the columns were replaced in their original positions. And, when it was considered that there were no further treasures to be found, the area was concreted over.

Ramses II sitting at the head of the courtyard named after him

The next sight to overwhelm us was the Hypostyle Hall with its thicket of thirty-two enormous columns arranged in four rows of eight, and characteristically endowed with figures and cartouches that belonged to Ramses II, Ramses IV, VI and Seti I. The Hall was the first inner room of the temple itself, and had served as a vestibule. Originally, it had been enclosed with a roof, but like the rest of the structures in the complex, it was open to the sky and of course to the bright sunlight which helped to highlight the figures carved on the columns. It was a delight to see that some of the original colours around the base of the capitals had survived, even though some of them had become a little fainter over the centuries. On either side of the rear wall were reliefs showing Amenhotep making offerings to the gods. However, between the last two columns, the Romans had erected an altar to the Emperor Constantine before he was converted to Christianity, and this could be seen from the central aisle.

A columned portico then led us to into the Sanctuary of Amun which was a central chamber flanked on either side by the barque shrines of Mut and Khonsu, whose statues were also brought in procession into the temple during the Opet Festival. The central chamber had, however, been encroached upon by the Romans who had plastered over the pharaonic reliefs in the third century and turned it into a cult church with paintings of their Emperors. Fragments of these paintings could still be seen at the top of the walls, and where the plaster had broken away, it exposed the original reliefs showing Amenhotep making offerings to Amun. Beyond lay the Hall of Offerings which had two columns each on either side of a central aisle to form a square, and to the right of it was the Birth Room of Amenhotep III where the reliefs told the legend of Amenhotep's divine birth when Thoth led Amun disguised as Amenhotep's father, to his mother's bedchamber. There were additional scenes of Isis presenting the child to Amun, and the sun god then cradling his son. These were explained by accompanying hieroglyphic texts one of which explained Amenhotep's birth by stating "his (Amun's) dew filled her body".

Adjoining the Birth Room was the Sanctuary of Amun's Barque, another holy room, for which its acacia doors were said to have been inlaid with gold. When Alexander the Great visited the temple, he decided to rebuild the Sanctuary by removing four columns and installing a granite shrine on which the sacred barque of Amun was placed after it had entered the temple. He also filled its walls with paintings of himself as pharaoh, and some of these had survived.

The very last chamber in the temple, being the Sanctuary of Amenhotep III, was considered the most sacred chamber of all where the gold statute of Amun was kept. Although badly damaged, the chamber still had the remains of the stone base on which the statue had stood. Its walls were covered with picturesque scenes and hieroglyphic texts that reached the ceiling, and it was a joy to see some of the original colours.

Exit was by the world famous Avenue of Sphinxes, an addition to the Temple which the 30th Dynasty monarch Nectanebo I (between 664-332 BC), had created. These two lines of female headed statues had once formed a glorious processional avenue between the temple and the one at Karnak, two miles away.

Nearby was the tiny restored Roman Temple of Seraphis, that had been installed by the Roman Emperor, Hadrian, on his birthday in AD 126. Seraphis was a god invented by the Ptolemies, being a combination of the Greek god Apis and the Egyptian god, Osiris. There were obvious signs of destruction with only some of its original columns standing to denote that it had once been a fine structure with a pillared forecourt. Worship had taken place in front of the statue, left headless inside the only room that was visible. The drapery on the statue instantly marked it as Roman.

With the line of palm trees towering behind the sphinxes, the Avenue provided a fitting exit from the site. It had been a magical visit, having enabled us to travel through several dynasties and seeing their own characteristic styles of architecture. As we turned the corner, there was something compelling about those towering structures that wanted us to go back.

The most audacious excavation taking place in Luxor today, is the attempt to uncover the entire length of the 3km long Avenue of Sphinxes in all its glory. By August 2010, two large sections had already been revealed, one of which was in the centre of Karnak village where some of its shops and dwellings had disappeared as a result of the excavations. Not surprisingly, some of the sphinxes looked a little worse for wear after their long burial, but it was hoped that the entire Avenue would have been resurrected by 2011, thus giving the world an insight as to how it had looked at the time of the pharaohs when it linked two of the greatest temples in that era.

The Temple of Seraphis

Present excavations in the centre of Karnak Village to find the continuation of the Avenue of Sphinx

KARNAK: THE TEMPLE OF AMUN

In ancient times, the spectacular temple complex of Karnak, 2 miles north of Luxor, was once linked to the Temple of Luxor by a processional avenue lined with sphinxes, and was the scene of great religious ceremonies and festivals, especially the holy festival of Opet which was shared with the temple of Luxor.

The original sanctuary of the temple was built during the Middle Kingdom period (2055-1650 BC during the 11th – 14th Dynasties), but work continued for the next 1,500 years when successive pharaohs of the 18th and 19th Dynasties such as Hatshepsut, Amenhotep III, Tuthmosis III and Ramses II added their own individual contribution of style and brilliance.

The temple complex had been divided into three temple sites, each of which was dedicated to Amun, Mut and Montu, the local Theban warrior god. But of the three sites, the Amun Temple Enclosure was by far the largest and the most inspiring, built to gigantic proportions on a site that extended 100 acres, and enough room it was said, to accommodate ten cathedrals, or even half of Manhattan Island.

The Mut Temple Enclosure consisted of a Temple dedicated to Mut, a hypostyle hall and two courts, but the Temple was completely ruined, and was not included on the tourist trail. It was built by Amenhotep III who set up more than 700 Sekhmet statues in black granite, such as the one seen at the British Museum. And, as noted at his Mortuary Temple, he also included an enormous number of the lioness goddess to accompany those of his own. It was thought that this extraordinary number of statues represented some sort of calendar; two for every day of the year, and to whom offerings had been made. An extraordinary find there during excavations in 1817 by the explorer/archaeologist, Belzoni, was the complete head of a red granite colossus, at first attributed to Tuthmosis III, but now thought to be that of Amenhotep III. It was found in front of the Temple of Khonspakhered, with part of the statue protruding through the ground. The head measured 3.1m (10ft) from the top of the mitre to the chin, and an arm, also found with the head, measured 7m (18ft) long.

Following its find, the head was stored in a private house in Cairo until Henry Salt saw it and acquired it and the arm for the British Museum. As the head was so heavy, Belzoni and his partner Beechey, took eight days to take it the 1 km to Luxor. This seemed an extraordinarily long time, and it was strange that they did not have the assistance of the dozens of carts that must have been about that time. Perhaps they had not been strong enough.

The Enclosure of Montu was situated to the west of the Amun Enclosure, and it too did not seem to attract many tourists. The ruins were in a bad state and access was difficult anyway. The main temple there had been erected by Amenhotep III and was dedicated to the falcon-headed Montu, who was one of the original deities of Thebes.

But it was to the great expanse of the Amun Enclosure that everyone was making their way, and no better place, since Karnak had become the most important place of worship in all of Egypt during the height of Theban power, and the pharaohs of the time acknowledged that it was the ideal place to set up temples to their divine god. And Karnak itself was growing into a wealthy town.

At the time of Ramses III, Karnak had expanded into sixty-five villages with over 400 gardens, kilometres of fields with over 42,000 head of cattle and a fleet of eighty-three ships. And in this great centre there were also 81,322 workers and slaves, 80,000 of which were engaged on the building of the great temple.

Since the first excavation in the mid nineteen century, Karnak became the greatest archaeological site outside the Pyramids of Giza, with its First Pylon measuring twice the size of the one at Luxor, and the largest in Egypt.

Entry into the temple complex was through a very modern pavilion built in 2008 which displayed a model of the entire area including some artefacts that 'set the scene'. At one time entry had been through the ticket office at the top of the Luxor corniche, a short taxi ride from the centre of the town, so it was a surprise in the March of 2010 to find that the enormous area that had once led to the temple, had been re-surfaced with marble paving and landscaped with trees surrounded by flower beds to create an ultra modern entrance. It had also created a much longer walk to the First Pylon which gave access into the temple enclosure.

At the far end of the concourse, a wooden bridge crossed the dried up remains of an ancient dock which had been part of the canal connecting the temple to the Nile, and from where the gold image of Amun had sailed in its sacred barge on visits from the Temple of Luxor to Karnak during the Festival of Opet. The dock had deteriorated into a deep craggy ditch which necessitated the bridge, and gave access into the temple's precinct. In ancient times, the canal had been flanked by the Avenue of Ram-headed Sphinxes which also provided a modern processional way into the temple. The much photographed rams were a creature sacred to Amun and were shown sheltering a small statue of Ramses II between their front paws. They ultimately led us towards the First Pylon, thought to have been built around the time of Nectanebo I of the 30th Dynasty, in the fourth century BC. Its walls were perfectly plain and had not been carved with any scenes as at other temples, and although it had not been completed, the Pylon measured 43m (129ft) high, 113m (339ft) wide and 15m (45ft) thick, undoubtedly making it the largest in Egypt. It certainly made a monumental entrance and gave a stunning first impression as to what lay ahead.

Karnak: The Avenue of Ram-headed sphinxes leading to the First Pylon

Having entered the enormous open area of the Forecourt between the First and Second Pylons, referred to as the Ethiopian Courtyard, we were immediately dazzled by the sight of the 15m (45ft) high statue of Ramses II dominating the top end. A book acquired at the site named the statue as being of Pinedjem, a pharaoh of the 21st Dynasty, and a high priest of Amun, but as he was not of the era when the Temple Enclosure was built, then the statue was more probably that of Ramses II, whose influence was to be seen all over the enclosure. Carved out of pink granite, its presence was highlighted by the fact that it was standing alone and not obscured by any other structures. An unusual feature was the little statue of his queen, Nefertari standing between his legs. This was also the case at Abu Simbel when Ramses had his family standing beside him on the façade. Close by stood the enormous column of the Pavillion of Taharka, an Ethiopian king, who built the pavilion, 21m (63ft) high, with a wooden roof to house the sacred boats. There was also another encounter with ram-headed sphinxes which had been placed along the bottom of the papyrus-budded columns and lying down each side of the Court. They had originally been commissioned by Ramses II to flank the entrance to the Hypostyle Hall, but had been moved to their present positions. Many of them had been damaged and were missing their heads, but it was obvious from their haphazard alignment that was not their original place.

To the right of the colossus and Column, and abutting the Court was the Temple of Ramses III, whose pylon was flanked by two statues of the pharaoh. Inside, the walls of its Festival Hall were lined on two sides with the Osiride figures of Ramses standing against each column, and making a powerful statement from the past. There were also two more figures of him standing on either side of the doorway leading to a small vestibule with four columns and ultimately leading to a smaller hypostyle hall with eight columns. At the far end of this 60m (180ft) long temple, Ramses had built three shrines in which the sacred barques of the Theban gods had rested during the religious celebrations performed there. But there was scaffolding in place for on-going restoration work which prevented people from seeing the hieroglyphs covering their walls.

Behind the colossus of Ramses II was a colonnade that marked the top end of the Court and fronted the Second Pylon. It was not as large as the First Pylon, and had been built by Horemheb, an 18th Dynasty general who had become the last pharaoh of that dynasty. On his death, it was completed by

Seti I of the 19th Dynasty. Both Seti's father, Ramses I, and his son, Ramses II, added their names to the wall as well as expounding their exploits above those of Horemheb.

The statue of Ramses' Queen Nefertari standing between the legs of his colossus

The inner courtyard of Ramses III's Temple

The Ethiopian Courtyard

If we had been overawed by the structures of the Courtyard, then we were in for an even greater thrill on entering the iconic and also much photographed Hypostyle Hall, consisting of a forest of 134 decorative columns with their open papyrus shaped capitals reaching 34m(102ft) high and dwarfing everyone passing beneath them. We were mesmerized by the size of the columns which also had a circumference of 15m (45ft), large enough to enable twelve people with extended arms to encircle them. It was also amazing to see the massive blocks of the architraves balancing on top of the columns overhead. At this point, we amusingly recalled the scene from the Agatha Christie film *Death on the Nile* when one of these blocks had been made to fall and kill a character. But we had no worries. They had remained there safely for well over three millennia! The size of the space making up the Hall was also staggering to comprehend. It covered an area of 6,000m (18,000ft) and, it was said, was large enough to contain both the Cathedrals of St.Peter's in Rome, and St.Paul's in London.

The Hall was the creation of Amenhotep III around 1375 BC, who had intended it to be just a simple colonnade leading towards the Sanctuary of Amun, but it was extended by Seti I and then by Ramses II, who also added the sunken reliefs. The bright morning sunshine cast diagonal shadows across the interior to accentuate the deep carvings, and brought them to life as well as the colour of the stonework. At one time the Hall had been brightly painted. It was just possible to glimpse some of the original colours around the capitals and on the undersides of the architraves which gave an idea how splendid it must have looked in Amenhotep's days.

The Third Pylon, built by Amenhotep III, ended the section occupied by the Hypostyle Hall, and marked the entrance into a narrow court in which Tuthmosis I had raised a pair of obelisks, in front of the Fourth Pylon, 23m (69ft) high and weighing 143 tons. This had marked the actual entrance into the temple at the time of his reign, but only one obelisk had been left standing. It was visible through an archway leading from the Fourth Pylon. Later, Ramses IV and VI, added their own cartouches to the monument. Even Tuthmosis III (1479-1425 BC), raised a pair in this area, but neither of them had survived. Their shattered remnants lay among the debris of other shattered buildings.

Beyond the Fourth Pylon, the temple became the realm of Tuthmosis III, who had purposely built his Hypostyle Hall around the two magnificent rose granite obelisks that Queen Hatshepsut had erected in order to hide

The Grand Columns of Amenhotep III's Courtyard

Restoration work in the Sanctuary of Amun

them and erase her name from the temple. But his 25m (75ft) high Hall could not hide the elegance of her 29m (77ft) high obelisks which she had commissioned from the granite quarries of Aswan to celebrate the sixtieth year of her reign, and which she had erected to "the glory of her father Amun". Hatshepsut had also included a text down the length of the monument, and it was this text that had assisted historians to learn more about her reign. Sadly, only one obelisk had survived. It was the tallest one in Egypt, and was estimated to have weighed 320 tons. However, the top portion of the one that had toppled over had survived its fall, and was on show for everyone to see its carving.

Behind the Hypostyle Hall lay the Fifth Pylon which was the work of Tuthmosis I, but there was very little space left between it and the Sixth Pylon, built by Tuthmosis III. It was the smallest in Karnak. In the vestibule beyond, Tuthmosis III had erected two granite columns on which had been carved the two emblems of Egypt; the water lily of Upper Egypt, and the Papyrus of Lower Egypt. Nearby, the statues of Amun and his female counterpart Amunet had been placed there at the time of Tutankhamun. Tuthmosis III also built a Sanctuary to take the sacred barque of Amun during the religious festivals. This was later replaced by a granite one by Alexander the Great (332-323 BC), and the reliefs painted by his successor and half brother Philip Arrhidaeus were all found to have been well preserved. Arrhidaeus was also shown making offerings to Amun.

To the left of the Sanctuary, Tuthmosis III had covered one wall displaying his victories over Hatshepsut's existing reliefs. He had also replaced her image and substituted his father's and grandfather's cartouches, (Tuthmosis I and Tuthmosis II). For a time, the chamber was shut so that restoration work could be carried out, and this was successfully completed.

Next, was a colonnaded courtyard surrounded with Osiride statues of the pharaoh. The item of interest there was the inscribed outer face of the pylon known as the Wall of Records on which were detailed the list of people Tuthmosis III had conquered during his military campaigns. The list was divided into two, showing the Nubians on the right and the Asiatics on the left. A text also extolled his victory at Megiddo (Armageddon) in 1479 BC.

Beyond the Shrine was the large Central Court which was thought to have been the site of the original temple built during the 12th Dynasty, but nothing of it had survived except for the three large rectangular bases of some kind of structure which had occupied its centre. Then, facing us at the top end was the Great Festival Hall of Tuthmosis III whose elongated façade of seven pillars on either side of a central doorway was similar in style to Seti I's Mortuary Temple at Abydos. The Temple, also known as Tuthmosis' "Mansion of a Million Years" was lying in ruins, but its interior contained several delightful sections flanked by papyrus-budded columns with their architraves still balancing on top of them. The thirty-two columns of the Festival Hall had been designed to imitate tent poles, a reference to Tuthmosis' life under canvas when he was away on his military campaigns. However, their capitals had been decorated with blue and white chevrons, and their architraves were also brightly coloured. Originally, the Hall had been painted dark red to imitate wood. As some Christian symbols were found on some of the columns, it was thought that the Hall had been used as a church. Tuthmosis III also added a small shrine at the back of the temple, on either side of which were the enormous bases on which two more of Hatshepsut's obelisks had stood.

A magnificent red granite statue, thought to be of Tuthmosis III, and acquired by the British Museum in 1823 from Henry Salt, was probably found in this area during the excavations in the early nineteenth century. And apart from the loss of the lower legs and the left arm, the rest of the statue, standing about 3m (9ft) high, was well preserved, and has been a striking exhibit at the Egyptian Centre in the Museum ever since.

Another interesting part of the temple was the columned vestibule referred to as the Botanical Gardens where there were scenes of exotic plants and flowers said to have been brought back to Egypt during Tuthmosis III's travels.

Ramses II also set his stamp here by building a set of shrines called the Temples of the Hearing Ear, and so called because they were decorated with carved ears. However, the little shrines became less approachable as they had been finally cut off by the surrounding wall.

Again, a base was found that had supported an obelisk which Ramses II had usurped from Tuthmosis III. This particular obelisk, and the tallest ever known at 32.2m (96.6ft), was destined for Constantinople on the orders of Emperor Constantine (AD 306-337), but was re-directed to Rome to stand in the Circus Maximus. However, in 1588, Pope Sixtus V had another idea, and ordered the obelisk to be re-erected in front of the Church of St. John (Giovanni) Lateran, where it has finally resided. This obelisk would have had a twin standing next to it, and was thought to have been the abandoned Unfinished Obelisk at Aswan which was rejected when flaws were found in the stone, and left where it had been carved in the quarry. The fact that it was left behind had given Egyptologists vital clues as to how these great structures had been created and lifted from the bed rock.

Having reached the far end of this "western" side of the Amun Temple Enclosure, there was still lots waiting to be seen on its "eastern" side, access to which was as far back as the Third Pylon where the Temple's secondary axis branched off from the main complex and ultimately led to the Sacred Lake lying to the east.

We retraced our steps back to the Third Pylon to where the great statue of Ramses II was also situated, and entered a large open spaced court, called the Cachette Court, so named as this was where a staggering 17,000 stone and bronze statues were found buried after excavating the site in 1903. On either side were half walls made up of odd blocks of stone that had obviously come from destroyed buildings, and which had been gathered by the archaeologists to form a kind of walkway towards the Seventh Pylon. However, the wall on the right contained blocks of hieroglyphs that had been perfectly matched next to each other and were all clearly highlighted by the sun's shadows.

The Hieroglyphs along 'Cachette Way'

The Sacred Lake

Further along lay the Eighth Pylon, built by Hatshepsut, and the oldest part of this north-south axis. There had been six colossi mounted there, including one of Amenhotep I, but none had survived. As we ventured further along, the entire area was very sandy underfoot, and looked very desolate with only half walls and narrow openings that had once given access into what had once been the Jubilee Temple of Amenhotep II. An odd assortment of statues, some in a good condition, had been placed against these half walls, and gave the impression of some kind of open air museum. It would have been far more interesting had some kind of identification been placed against them so we could have known who they were, nevertheless they contributed to the mystique of the area. Just above a pathway, a few Osiride figures that had graced an inner courtyard gave us some indication as to how this structure must have looked, even though they were missing their heads.

Some statues discovered during the late 20th Century excavations

The ruins suddenly gave way to an even greater open space where the immensity of the Temple enclosure became very obvious with the Sacred Lake situated in its centre, and what a glorious sight it made with the palm trees rising above its eastern shores. Even the Lake had enormous proportions, measuring 120m (360ft) by 77m (221ft). At one time it had been fed by water channelled from the Nile, and was where the priests bathed before commencing their rituals every morning. Their homes and the remains of the Temple's storehouses lay in crumbled ruins around the edges of the lake. There had even been an aviary for aquatic birds, and a Nilometer to guage the level of the Nile. Across the way, rose the surviving pylons of the Temple and the great walls of Tuthmosis III's Festival Hall, with the obelisks of Tuthmosis I and Hatshepsut rising even higher.

Close by was a gigantic Scarab Beetle carved out of red granite and squatting on top of a high plinth. This had been erected by Amenhotep III as a dedication to Aten, the disc of the rising sun. People encircling the statue, once for good luck, three times for marriage and seven times in the hope of a first child, made a strange sight. But it was to the shaded awnings of the Café that people were largely making their way where cooling refreshments were to be had, and thus refreshed, it was time to keep our rendezvous with the coach. But before making our exit through the First Pylon, the gigantic statue of Ramses II gave us an unforgettable and lasting impression as we passed it on the way out.

THE TEMPLE OF HATHOR: DENDERA

As Dendera had not appeared on our itinerary, we found to our surprise that by the time we had finished breakfast the next morning, we had sailed over 30 miles north of Luxor and had moored at the quayside of Qena. There, coaches were waiting to take us to the temple located at the far end of the town bustling with morning shoppers. Ever since the security alert, all boats were moored in a specially guarded zone and passengers taken to the temples in a convoy with armed checkpoints along the way manned by armed security police.

The temple, dedicated to the universal mother goddess Hathor, was begun during the reign of the Macedonian king Ptolemy IX in 125 BC, long after the pharaohs of Egypt had died out. The Ptolemies succeeded Alexander the Great who ruled Egypt after his conquest, and on his death, Ptolemy, his favourite general was pronounced king. It was his successors who embraced the Egyptian mythology and built temples in the old style down the Nile Valley from Luxor to Aswan, the route all Nile cruises follow.

Dendera was the northernmost of the Ptolemaic temples in Upper Egypt and the last great religious foundation of ancient Egypt. When the pagan cults of ancient Egypt had gradually died out between the third century BC and the fifth century AD, the Greek kings of the Ptolemaic Dynasty kept many aspects of the ancient religion alive, and although they continued to build temples to the old floor plan, they added their own influence to the architectural details.

The temple had also been partially built by the Romans during the reign of Tiberius in AD 35, who added their own style of columns by omitting the great pylons that once graced their entrances. Their artists also drew the female figure in a different manner, for whilst the Egyptians had drawn their women in a more modest manner fully robed, the Romans adopted a more erotic style by portraying the goddesses with exposed breasts which were greatly emphasised when all the figures were seen from a side viewpoint.

Although the Romans had given a pylon-shaped façade to this particular temple, they added six columns topped with the goddesses' head instead of the traditional lotus shaped ones. The entire complex also included a sacred lake and several small shrines which extended the entire area to some 40,000sq.m (120,000sqft). The Roman builders also enclosed it with a tall mud-brick wall as a protective measure against the annual floods. And, whilst the temple was in a perfect state of preservation, the outside shrines were lying in ruins with only some of their walls still standing.

Hathor was portrayed as a woman with the ears of a cow and had the sun disc above her head inside a pair of horns. She was known as the goddess of love and harmony, with one of her symbols being the musical instrument called the sistrum (a small hand instrument with wires and small discs that rattled when shook), and as she also represented the cosmos in which all life took form, the temple was conceived as one enormous instrument in which the harmonies of the cosmos were brought together. In this respect her temple also became known as the Sistrum Temple. During the Greco-Roman period Hathor was as equally popular as the Roman goddess Venus. The falcon headed god Horus, as consort to Hathor, was also widely featured around the temple. His statuette was brought to the temple each year for one night of reunion with Hathor, and this meeting of the two gods was widely celebrated at Dendera, and similarly at Edfu, whenever Hathor journeyed there by barge to be reunited with Horus, or visa versa. Both were treated as though they were living people.

After stepping down from the coaches, we found ourselves in an enormously large empty space fringed with palm trees and enough room to park dozens of coaches and cars. Our first glimpse of the temple was from a distance, and our first impressive encounter was the ruined Monumental Gateway that had been built for the Roman emperors Trajan and Domitan in the first century. It looked enormously tall standing alone with no supporting walls and, interestingly, had inscribed figures at its base showing the Roman Emperor Domitan, wearing the high domed crown of Egypt and offering a glass of wine to both Hathor and Horus. In front of the base was the statue of a recumbent lion, but most of its face had withered away.

En route to Dendera: Qena Village on the West Bank

The Roman Gateway

Beyond the Gateway, a long paved causeway then led us to the temple to the left of which were the ruins of a building that had decorative Corinthian columns, but the façade of Hathor's temple was much plainer with six columns, three on either side of the central doorway and linked by decorative screens covered with hieroglyphs. The carved head of Hathor decorated the top of each column. Once inside, the inner courtyard was surrounded by columns again decorated with Hathor's face and all glowing pink in the bright morning sunshine. Between the columns the screen walls had been richly inscribed with figures showing both the Roman emperors Tiberius and Claudius, offering gifts to Hathor and Horus.

From the courtyard we entered the rather dimly lit Outer Hypostyle Hall, with its high roof supported by two rows of nine columns which tended to take up the floor space, but on looking up, we were rewarded with a ceiling dominated by astronomical signs and symbols featuring Nut, as goddess of the sky stretching across it, and with the hours of the night represented by animals and men forming a distinctive pattern, and the hours of daylight represented by twelve boats in which stood a god or goddess. The ceiling had been severely blackened from the fires of those who had inhabited the temple, but in 2008, scaffolding had been erected to enable the affected areas to be cleaned. Happily, this procedure had successfully revealed the original colours which had miraculously survived the grime of centuries. Most pleasing were the blues, rose and turquoise colours that lifted the figures and accentuated the brilliance of the artists who had drawn and painted them. Following this make-over, the ceiling deserved the honour of being the finest and the best preserved in Egypt. No matter where we went, the walls of the temple appeared to be covered with hieroglyphic texts telling the story of the temple's construction. There were also panels of fine carvings that fully illustrated it, starting with the traditional marking out of the boundaries which was performed by the pharaoh and the royal goddess Seshat who was holding the measuring tape and recording the details on a palm stalk. The panels ran like a picture book along the walls, and it was possible to follow the proceedings as they took place. It was fascinating to witness the perfection of the carvings with every recurring figure carved exactly as its predecessor with not a millimetre in deviation. How this was achieved was incredible to believe, but this was the magic of Egypt, where such marvellous artwork appeared everywhere, proving what incredible skills the ancient Egyptians had.

The Hathor-headed columns of the Courtyard

The restored paintings in the Hypostyle Hall ceiling, showing Isis and Nephtys protecting the body of Osiris

At the far end of the Hall was the entrance to the Inner Hypostyle Hall, which had just two rows of three columns on either side of a central walkway.

Again, the face of Hathor looked down on us from the top of the columns where traces of the original blue colour was clearly visible. The walls there were also covered with decorative panels that continued to tell the story of the foundation rituals, one of which showed the Pharaoh breaking the ground with an enormous hoe. Another distinctive panel featured Ptolemy IX, wearing the Crown of Egypt and surmounted by two tall feathers, offering what looked like two small jars as gifts to the seated Hathor and Horus. In this picture Horus was also shown wearing the double feathers instead of the double crown with which he was usually associated.

On either side of the Hall were six small chambers where all the regalia for the sacred rituals had been kept. Each room had its own function, one of which stored wine and food for offerings. But in the chamber where perfume and incense had been stored, the walls were covered with recipes for mixing the ingredients. There was a library too where all the religious texts had been stored. Interestingly, its doorway was framed with the temple's calendar, but as its interior was extremely dark, it was not possible to view the hieroglyphs inside. It was also extremely small, being just as large as an ordinary walk-in cupboard. There was also a little Treasury for storing the jewels and precious stones for presenting to the goddess, and lastly, a special chamber where the ceremonial vestments had been kept.

There was one wall in the vicinity that attracted a great deal of attention, namely the panels which featured a barefooted Hathor suckling her son Ihy and looked upon by Horus wearing the domed crown and appearing as a young naked boy with a finger pointing towards his mouth. Both Ihy and Horus were featured with shaved heads – the fashion for young boys at that time, except for a lock of hair which hung down over one ear. It was interesting to note that the artist had provided Hathor with an attractive diagonal design on her full length dress, which was obviously a Romanised fashion statement of what women were wearing in first century Egypt. Her headdress had also been given an intricate pattern which included folded wings.

Next to the Hypostyle Hall was another much smaller room called the Hall of Offerings. This room had no columns and was where altars had been installed and filled each day with offerings of food for the goddess, but which were later consumed by the priests themselves.

As we proceeded further into the temple, the rooms became smaller and darker, and beyond the Hall of Offerings lay a small vestibule that led directly into The Sanctuary, the holiest room in the temple where the golden statuette of Hathor had been kept along with the sacred barge that had carried her on ceremonial occasions. The wooden barge, about 3m (9ft) long, stood on a tall pedestal in the centre of the room, and was a good replica of the original which had been taken away to the British Museum. Not surprisingly, the statuette of Hathor was not in its niche at the back of the room, and there was no record as to what had happened to it.

The Sanctuary itself was a separate structure within the temple, with its own walls and its own massive doorway that reached the ceiling. Originally, it had two bronze doors, but these were missing. In the past they had always been kept locked and the room left in constant darkness. It was only lit whenever the pharaoh, who was the only person to be admitted inside, went to pay homage to Hathor. And it was always left locked whenever Horus paid his yearly visit to Hathor and left alone with her for the night.

The Sanctuary was also surrounded by a narrow corridor, with the one on the left occupied by several tiny chambers set against the outer walls of the temple. They had also served as storerooms, except for the one immediately behind the Sanctuary holding a second statuette of Hathor. Leading off the Vestibule in front of the Sanctuary was a short corridor on the right which led to another self contained structure within the temple called a *Wabet* and known as The New Year Chapel. This was where offerings to the goddess were made before carrying her up to the roof on each New Year's Day to be rejuvenated by the rays of the rising run. This ceremony was also a symbolic meeting between her and the sun god, and where she was shown to the people who had clamoured to see her. As goddess of love, the sight of Hathor was thought to have brought them luck in their marital affairs. The entrance to the Chapel was up some rather worn looking stone steps flanked on either side by a Hathor headed column, and on entering, a pleasant surprise was the spectacular painting spread across its ceiling showing the goddess Nut giving birth to the sun which was then showering Hathor with its golden rays. It was amazing to see that the original blue and gold colours had survived the surrounding grime.

Once through the Chapel, a curving staircase led us up to the roof. But, as it was dimly lit, with the only light coming through tiny windows positioned at each turn , care had to be exercised in mounting them. Along the way, we could see that the walls were covered with scenes depicting the jollity of the occasions as Hathor was borne upwards to the roof followed by musicians and dancers.

The New Year Chapel

The ceiling detail of Hathor's rejuvenation by the Sun
by kind pernission of Mr Neil Carpenter

Relief of King offering Hathor symbol of divinity with Horus in attendance

Once on top, Hathor was conducted to the little Chapel of the Union with the Sun Disc which had survived intact for everyone to admire. This was where the rejuvenation ceremony was carried out. Roofless, the Chapel consisted of twelve columns forming a square, and were again surmounted with the head of Hathor with carved screens in between.

Sharing the roof space were two other small chapels or shrines where the mysteries of Osiris were celebrated. The shrines were known as the tombs of Osiris, since it was at Dendera that one of his body parts was found after being scattered by his brother Seth. Both had small courtyards, and in one there were reliefs showing priests attending Osiris' funeral, and had texts telling how he brought dead matter back to life. The courtyard of the other chapel located on the opposite side of the roof was similar to the first, but the most interesting feature of this chapel was a circular zodiac sign stretching across the ceiling of the vestibule. This was a masterpiece of ancient art showing the festive days of the year with gods and goddesses holding up an inner circle crammed with human figures and animals representing the twelve signs of the zodiac. The zodiac was introduced into Egypt by the Romans who had acquired it from the Babylonians. This particular zodiac was dated to approximately 305 BC, but unfortunately, it had been blackened with age, and it had just been possible to see that the outer circle with its goddesses creating an attractive pattern. Alas, it was a plaster copy. The original had been cut away by art collectors who had then given it to the Louvre in Paris.

There had been another staircase, rather straighter than the first, and down which Hathor was taken back to her Sanctuary, but after retracing our steps down the curving one, we were conducted to the crypt where one chamber was open to visitors. In all, there were a series of crypts in which the most sacred relics and cult emblems had been kept, but as some relics had been stolen in the past, the authorities allowed only one crypt to be visited at any one time under the supervision of an authorised guide, and admission was limited to a small group. But as each crypt was tiny anyway and space extremely limited, the restriction in numbers was reasonable. The entrance was also restrictive and required some bending, but once inside, there was a wealth of carvings to admire. The chamber was softly illuminated by a series of foot lights along the floor, and these gave a warm golden glow to the carvings. Especially noteworthy, were the exquisitely carved duck and ibis among the birds featured in the lower panels.

The Little Temple of Isis

Back outside in the brilliant sunshine, we found ourselves in a wide open air corridor set in between the external and the outer protective walls. There, we were confronted with a myriad of hieroglyphics covering the exterior walls and felt at a great disadvantage in not being able to decipher the stories they told. There had been a large carving of Hathor's head in the centre of the wall, and although it had been badly defaced, it was an interesting feature with Hathor flanked by two other goddesses. The exterior wall also gave us a striking relief of Cleopatra holding a sistrum alongside her son Ceasarion holding incense, as offerings to Hathor. This image of Cleopatra was said to have been the only one of her to be seen in Egypt. She was the daughter of the last Ptolemaic monarch, Ptolemy XI, and she herself was the last queen of Egypt, who on her death in 30 BC at the age of thirty-eight, ended the Ptolemaic Dynasty.

Outside, there were several ruined structures which had featured in the temple's history, the first being the Temple of Isis which lay to the north of the temple, but it had been badly defaced by the Christians before it had fallen into ruin.

On the eastern side, lay the Sacred Lake. This was where the priests bathed each morning before they started their religious duties, and was surrounded by a small protective wall. Water was channelled in directly from the Nile, but over the centuries it had entirely dried out and had become overgrown with a few palm trees which towered over the wall. The lake had also featured at the festivals celebrating the union of Hathor and Horus when both were ceremoniously set across the waters in their own individual barges.

To the south, lay the ruined shell of the Sanatorium. Its foundations had survived as had some walls to a height of a few feet which revealed a row of individual rooms situated around its external walls. Its inner rooms had also crumbled away to ground level. The Sanatorium was the place where the sick and the poor went to seek a cure from their ills by drinking the holy water that had been poured over Hathor's golden statue, or were given herbs and other natural remedies by the physician-priests. The Sanatorium had only recently come to light when it was discovered beneath the sand in the 1960s.

Next to the Sanatorium was the Mammisi built during the reign of the 30th Dynasty pharaoh Nectenebo I (380-362 BC) but was completed during the time of the Romans who had split it into two whilst building the protective walls. The little temple not only celebrated the birth of Ihy, Hathor's son, but held festivals to celebrate times of prosperity. Its interior walls told the story of Ihy's birth, and just inside the entrance, one relief showed the ram-headed god Khnum modelling the child on his potter's wheel. The innermost room showed Hathor suckling her young son.

Adjoining the birth house was the Christian Bascilica, built at the end of the first millennium, and the earliest of the Christian churches in Upper Egypt. It had been heavily incised with crucifixes; the Copts having made sure that they had put their mark on their place of worship to differentiate it from the surrounding pagan structures. This was pointed out to us with great pride by a long robed individual who had stationed himself at the exit.

A few metres beyond, lay the Roman Mammisi, located on the edge of the complex, and built alongside the outer protective wall at the time of the Roman emperor Augustus, probably at the beginning of the second century. It was built on a grander scale than Nectenebo's with a decorative façade comprising five Hathor-headed columns and carved screens in between. It also had an outer corridor for processions. The front of the temple had survived intact along with the roof, but the rest of the rectangular structure had almost disappeared except for a few crumbled walls that marked its outline. On top of each column was the figure of Bes, the grotesque looking god with large ears and an extended belly who protected all women in childbirth. Bes was also said to ward off all evil spirits, and was a favourite deity with young children who had adopted him as a good luck charm. We found an effigy of the happily smiling god on our way out including an undamaged head of Hathor carved on a single stone.

A parade of shops and an outside cafeteria tempted many tourists leaving the site, but as refreshments awaited us upon our arrival back at *The Nile Commodore*, we hurriedly returned to our waiting coaches.

Bes

ABYDOS: THE TEMPLE OF SETI I

This wonderful Mortuary Temple of Seti I, at Abydos, just north of Dendera, earned its right to be included among the other temples along the Nile, as it was considered to be among the most beautiful of the New Kingdom temples and the best preserved.

Abydos was considered to have been the most important religious site along the Nile and had been a place of pilgrimage for those wishing to be buried as close as possible to the symbolic tomb of Osiris, whose head, according to Egyptian mythology, had been found there after being dismembered by his brother Seth.

Thereafter, Abydos became a shrine to Osiris with pilgrims aspiring to visit his 'tomb' at least once in their lifetime, and with the creation of the Osirion, Osiris' fake tomb, Abydos maintained its importance for being a sacred burial site.

The cult of Osiris had formed part of the orthodox religion in ancient Egypt, and those who had visited the 'tomb' recorded that fact on the walls of their tombs to ensure their speedy passage to the afterlife.

The first temple to have been built at Abydos was around 3,200 BC, but Abydos had been an ancient burial site since the days of the First Dynastic kings, spanning 6,000 years where some 350 tombs were discovered, including the *mastabas* of the early pharaohs, which were in fact dummy tombs, built there so that their spirit or *ka* could also have a closer association with their lord of the underworld.

The Ancient Egyptians also brought their animals and birds to be buried at Abydos, many of which were those considered to be sacred, including jackals, who symbolised the god Anubis; ibises, which were the incarnation of Thoth, and falcons symbolising the falcon god Horus. In 2001, archaeologists even discovered the mummified remains of rodents, along with countless falcons.

The ancient Egyptians had a love affair with animals which they mummified in their thousands, however large or small. The most popular were cats and birds, but crocodiles, even hippopotami and bulls were mummified. Many of the animals, bulls in particular, were slaughtered in the temples and offered to the gods, and many mummified animals also found their way into the tombs. And, as discovered by the archaeologists, there were even those people who provided their pets with gold embellished coffins.

Realising how important Abydos was, Seti I, the son of Ramses I and the second ruler of the 19th Dynasty (1318-1304 BC), ordered the reconstruction of all its old buildings which had fallen into decay and took steps to preserve the sanctity of the site.

At one time, Abydos had also accommodated a large temple complex as well as sacred lakes, but everything had disappeared, and over time, the site became sanded over. The only three structures remaining were Seti's temple, the tomb of Osiris, called the Osirion, and the temple of Ramses II, lying some 400m (1200ft) to the west.

Built of both limestone and sandstone, the temple was dedicated to the six deities, Osiris, Horus, Isis, Amun, Ra-Horakhty, and Ptah-Sokar, and unlike any other temple, it was built to an unusual L-shaped design. (Sokar was another funerary god.)

Seti I was another prolific builder, his main achievements being his great temple at Karnak and this one at Abydos, but he died before the latter was completed, and the work was then undertaken by his son, Ramses II, who built its pylons, forecourts and its grand portico. Ramses also decorated the outer Hypostyle Hall although the artwork was not considered as good as the work produced at the time of his father, nevertheless they were decorative and told their own stories.

Our first glimpse of the temple was its wide façade comprising twelve square columns, six on either side of the main door to form an elegant looking entrance. Leading up to the portico was a flight of broad steps with ramps in between, and at the top lay twelve large blocks of stone, which were the remnants of the second pylon, and which formed a boundary wall to the large paved area in front of the portico.

Abydos: The Facade of Seti I's Mortuary Temple

Seti I being purified with holy water by Horus (L), and Wepwawet the jackal-headed god of Assyut (R)

The columns along the portico had been decorated by Ramses who had included reliefs of his children; the girls on one side and the boys on the other, many of which were showing traces of their original colours. There were also inscriptions which recorded the historical fact that Ramses had visited Abydos during the first year of his reign.

The temple had also been built using the two most sacred numbers; two and seven in its construction, thereby giving it two pylons, two courtyards, and two Hypostyle Halls. There had also been seven doors leading into the temple, and seven chapels, all of which were dedicated to the six deities, including one for Seti himself. However, four of the seven doors had been blocked off during Ramses' time leaving only the central door to enter the temple.

The Outer Hypostyle Hall was the first to be entered. It was a large space but was split up by twenty-four papyrus headed columns which supported its roof and had been laid out in two rows of twelve. Topping the columns were papyrus shaped capitals. As elsewhere, its columns had been covered with hieroglyphs and cartouches of Seti I, but again, Ramses had asserted his presence by displaying himself killing his enemies on one column and worshipping Osiris on another. The Hall had also been decorated with scenes of Ramses in the presence of the six gods, but there was a delightful picture of Seti being purified by Osiris on his one side, and Horus on his other. There were also a series of beautifully carved panels showing the Nile god Hapi kneeling and holding a tray laden with gifts. He was said to represent the major cities through which the Nile flowed.

The Inner Hypostyle Hall was as large as the first and had twenty-four columns, twelve only of which had capitals representing lotus buds. It was the last part of the temple to have been completed by Seti before he died, and contained the most beautifully coloured reliefs ever seen in an Egyptian temple. The Hall had been delicately lit with a soft green light that gave the surroundings an ethereal ambience and brought to life the glorious colours. Most prominent were the scenes of Seti honouring the various gods.

At the far end of the Hall lay the seven individual sanctuaries which stretched the entire width of the temple and were composed of long narrow rooms, about 3m (9ft)wide. Each one was dedicated to the six gods, but one had also been reserved for Seti. In each sanctuary, the god's sacred barge had been kept. With the exception of the Sanctuary of Osiris, all the others had a false door carved into the wall, but every one had been beautifully decorated with colourful scenes that glowed from their walls.

Left: The Shrine of Osiris – Seti I presenting the god with glasses of wine

There were also niches set into the walls in which a statue of a deity had been kept.

The first Sanctuary to attract our attention with its colours was the Sanctuary of Horus. There, its inside walls were richly decorated with images of Horus presenting the crowns of Egypt to Seti, with Isis touching him with the ankh to bring him long life and happiness. Recessed into the wall was a delightful niche which was also richly decorated and showed Seti offering gifts to a seated Osiris, wearing the high domed crown of Egypt. Again, soft lighting brought the colours alive.

Next, was the Sanctuary of Isis where the goddess was shown in scenes representing the daily life of the temple, such as opening the shrine door, being anointed and receiving gifts of incense.

Next door was the Sanctuary of Osiris, considered to be the most important one in the temple. Its ceiling was also unusual, having been made out of red granite. Its recessed shrine showed Seti I presenting gifts to Osiris who this time was wearing the crown with the two tall feathers. As we passed from one Sanctuary to another, it was amazing to see the excellence of the reliefs as they told their own stories.

Apart from these individual shrines, there were also individual chapels dedicated to Horus, Isis, and Osiris, the most decorative of which was the Chapel to Horus with its enormous picture of Seti handing the seated Horus with the royal sceptre in the presence Isis. The ancient artists certainly had an eye for colour. Again, the rich browns of the figures contrasted with the blue colours of Seti's crown and Horus' blue feathered headdress along with the turquoise of his garments. The figure of Isis was in yellow, as was her crown of two tall feathers, but the decorative red bow tied around her waist looked very striking against the white of her pleated dress. The artists had even incorporated red and blue into the folds of Seti's kilt to match the other colours of the tableau.

Leading off the second Hypostyle Hall to the left was a long passageway called the Gallery of Kings. There were no colours to be seen there only two large carvings which covered its grey walls showing Seti and his son Ramses II pointing to the long line of seventy-six cartouches which represented the names of every one of their ancestors from the First Dynastic pharaoh Menes onwards. This unique list had, apparently, assisted historians greatly in putting the rulers in their correct chronological order, but strangely the names of Hatshepsut, Akenhaten, and Tutankhamun were missing. It had also come to the historian's attention that Seti had recorded his name as *Menmare Osiris-Merneptah* instead of *Menmare Seti-Merneptah*, probably to distance himself from his namesake Seth who had murdered Osiris.

Turning left, lay the Hall of Books which had probably been the library where all the religious texts had been stored. Next door was the Hall of Barques, and the Hall of Sacrifices where in the latter, the slaughter for the offerings had been carried out. Worth noting in the adjoining Corridor of Bulls was an interesting image of Ramses and his son Amun-her Khepsh-ef lassoing a bull, whilst on another wall, father and son were offering ducks to Amun-Ra and the goddess Mut. In this part of the temple the walls had not been coloured, and it had been difficult in the low light to capture the reliefs on film without the aid of flash photography which was strictly forbidden throughout the temple, so it was a matter of hoping for the best. In fact had a flash bulb gone off by mistake, an attendant was soon to complain.

We found an open door that led out into the sunshine and headed for the Osirion, Osiris' mythological tomb, which was discovered lying under a pile of rubble in 1902 by the English archaeologist Francfort.

The Osirion had been built by Seti I, using massive blocks of granite, but his grandson, Merenptah (Ramses II's thirteenth son who succeeded him), was responsible for the decorations.

The Osirion had been purposely built below ground level, as befitting the lord of the underworld, and contained several chambers including a flooded central one in which a sarcophagus had been placed in its centre to represent an island. This represented the land rising from the primeval waters of Creation, as a symbol of Osiris' rebirth.

As it was constantly flooded, the Osirion was considered too dangerous to enter. In any case, the prospect of climbing down appeared irksome and the stagnant water did not look inviting. And although a timbered staircase led down to its depths, no one ventured beyond the viewing platform. Red granite pillars had once held up the roof, but as they had collapsed, it was possible to see the internal layout of the central chamber, and how the surviving upright blocks had formed a rectangle of pillars. But as we were standing some distance away, we were not able to see the carvings that covered the chamber's eastern wall. We could see a doorway leading from it to connect with another room. And, although we could not appreciate the fact, the interior of the Osirion had also been richly decorated.

The long corridor that had once connected the old entrance to the

Osirion had been decorated with scenes from the Book of Gates and the Book of Caverns. And, at its end was a hall and a small room decorated with the figure of Merenptah paying homage to Osiris and Horus.

Another chamber had been decorated with astronomical scenes showing Nut, extending her body towards Geb, god of the earth. It was a shame that the Osirion was out of bounds. It had much to offer the observer.

TEMPLE OF RAMSES II

The final structure in the vicinity was the sad ruins of Ramses II's Temple which lay at the edge of Beni Mansur, a small village, some 400m (1200ft) to the west. By all accounts, it had once been magnificent and was said to have been one of the finest ever built by Ramses. It had been built with limestone, but its pillars were made from sandstone and its Sanctuary from alabaster. Ramses also used pink and black granite for the door frames.

Ramses had conformed to the usual plan by using two pylons with two courts and two hypostyle halls, and several chapels dedicated to various gods, the royal ancestors and one for himself.

And like at his Mortuary Temple on the West Bank, the outside walls had been decorated with scenes of Ramses telling his favourite story of his victory at the Battle of Qadesh. The second pylon had led into a peristyle court surrounded on all three sides by six Osirion pillars, but these had been severely damaged and the walls had only survived to a height of about 2m (6ft).

The walls of the interior had also been as beautifully decorated as his father's temple, and although only half their size remained, they nevertheless produced some stunning reliefs, all of which were painted in glowing colours. Had it not fallen into ruin, the temple could have rivalled that of his father's and given us another splendid journey into Egypt's ancient past.

Another amazing discovery made at Abydos in 1998, were two bone tablets containing a form of writing that hitherto had not been seen before. The writing preceded hieroglyphs and was considered to have been written by people who had lived around 3,400 BC when the first pharaohs had started to build their *mastabas* there. These historic tablets were considered to be the earliest known written documents to be found in Egypt.

The Osireion

ESNA: THE TEMPLE OF KHNUM

Back on board *The Nile Commodore*, we cruised thirty miles south of Luxor to arrive at the quayside Esna where our coaches were waiting to take us to the Temple of Khum, dedicated to the mythological ram-headed god who fashioned mankind on his potter's wheel from clay obtained from the Nile. He was also the principal deity worshipped at Esna.

The temple, situated on the eastern bank of the Nile, measured 450ft long, had been built during the Greco-Roman period under Ptolemy VI Philometor, over the ruins of an earlier temple built during the reign of Tuthmosis III (1479-1425 BC). The Romans, under the Emperor Marcus Aurelius (AD 121-180), also built a quay to connect the temple to the Nile.

When the temple was discovered in 1828 by Champollion, only the Hypostyle Hall, built during the reign of Claudius in the first century, was visible above the buildings of the town which had been built on top of it. So much so, that when Napoleon's troops arrived in the town, they were able to scratch their names on the top portions of the columns. Consequently, the Hypostyle Hall was the only part that could be successfully excavated when work commenced in the 1860s.

The town had been built over the ancient city of Latopolis, so called by the Greeks, as their word for the river's perch was *lates* which were represented by the goddess Neith, and she was also worshipped here. In ancient times, Esna had become a prosperous trading centre with roads linking the Nile Valley with the cities in the south, and was until the nineteenth century a port of call for camel caravans crossing the desert from Sudan. To the south of the town lay one of the supply routes to the gold mines of central Africa which brought such wealth to Egypt, and allowed the pharaohs of the 18th Dynasty to lavish such luxury upon their temples, and produce the magnificent structures we see today.

Esna was also situated just south of a sandstone dam built by British engineers in the form of two barrages across the Nile in 1906 to control its floods. The barrages also acted as bridges, and had locks to allow river traffic to flow through. These then gave the local trades people the opportunity of showing off their goods to the passing tourist boats. This was our experience as we waited to enter the lock, when several of them appeared with their carpets and shawls draped over their shoulders or along extended arms, and vying for our attention. They even unrolled a carpet or two to land on the top deck, but as we were on the move, we could not enter into any transactions with them. In a matter of minutes we had arrived at our mooring and set off for the very short ride to the temple.

On arrival, we found the temple in the middle of the town and about 9m (27ft) below ground level, but we were soon struck by the grandeur of its twenty-four columns that made up the single Hypostyle Hall, each of which had different capitals imitating the shapes of palm leaves, lotus plants and papyrus fans. Some had even been decorated with bunches of grapes which was purely of Roman influence. It was a delight to see the subtle shades of blues and pinks that had survived the grime of centuries.

Its façade though, had been a simple one, similar to Dendera, with six columns on either side of the entrance doorway and decorative screens in between. The façade had also been carved with the cartouches of three Roman Emperors: Claudius and Titus to the right, and Vespasian to the left.

Having entered its lofty interior, the Hall appeared to have been in two halves, with their own cluster of columns set out in three rows, describing the various festivals that had taken place there. One relevant inscription was devoted to quoting a hymn to Khnum, acknowledging him as creator of all. There was also an interesting relief of the Emperor Trajan offering a lotus flower to Khnum.

The names of Roman Emperors, Septimus Severus, Caracalla and Geta were also mentioned on the walls to the left, and the name of another, Decius was mentioned on the back of the northern wall to the right. There, he was seen making offerings to Khnum at his potter's wheel. Another showed the Emperor Commodus netting fish in the presence of Horus and Khnum, thus continuing the tradition of showing the monarchs in the presence of gods.

The back wall, which was the only remaining part of the original

Ptolemaic temple also had reliefs featuring two of the Ptolemaic rulers: Ptolemy VI Philometor, and Ptolemy VIII Euergetes. who were keen to show that they, like the rest of the dynasty, had embraced Egyptian culture.

The ceiling, although darkened with the dirt and neglect of centuries, was an interesting focal point with its astronomical theme featuring creatures of the zodiac, among which was a very large scorpion, but the gloom almost made identifying them difficult. The ceiling was said to rival that at Dendera for its detail and artistry. However, since a cleaning-up programme had already started, the ceiling should, one day, reveal its true beauty.

The outside walls contained texts dedicated to Emperor Marcus Aurelius with scenes depicting Emperors Titus, Domitian and Trajan, killing figures representing Egypt's enemies. However, Khnum had the last word: he was seen being worshipped as the creator of all things by various gods on the lintel of the back gateway.

After Roman times, the temple became a Christian church and then the town's granary. Thereafter, it was used as a cotton store when Esna became a centre for weaving cloth. Cotton from the surrounding areas was harvested between October and November, and it was said that practically the whole population participated in its harvest. Esna was still regarded as an agricultural and rural town. A picturesque boulevard of eucalyptus trees and sycamores lined the Nile and led to the busy market place. Because only the Hypostyle Hall had been excavated, it was disappointing that our visit had turned out to be a short one.

Upon returning to our Nile cruiser, we were again welcomed back with a refreshing and cooling glass of orangeade. This was the time when the temperature had begun to rise, making the sunshine less bearable when the sun was directly overhead. An aperitif before lunch was also an enjoyable experience especially when taken in the supreme comfort of the lounge bar on the penultimate deck. After lunch, the sun deck beckoned where comfortable chairs around tables set out in neat rows under an awning, afforded the best views of the passing landscape as we glided by.

The river banks were full of life, more so on the eastern side where young children were again part of the passing scene as they played along the banks; the young boys in particular appeared to have no fear of the water as they launched their small boats. They all waved excitedly as we passed which was probably why they were there, as the sight of a continuous procession of cruisers must have been part of their day.

One of our particular highlights was of course the four o'clock tea party on the top deck, so everyone waited for the gong that summoned us all there.

Another highlight was the evening's entertainment in the Salon after dinner. The Ancient Egyptian Evening proved very popular when everyone dressed up in colourful Egyptian dress and all looked authentically Arabic. The games included women binding their menfolk from head to foot with yards of toilet paper, and being given prizes for the best looking 'mummy'.

Such hilarity and exertion had extracted volumes of energy that none of us thought we had, and despite the temptation of staying up late, the anticipation of waking up to another exciting day gave everyone the incentive of getting off to bed.

All dressed up for our Gala Night

EDFU: THE TEMPLE OF HORUS

The appetising smell of freshly baked bread welcomed us yet again into the restaurant for breakfast the next morning; the bakers having been busy throughout the night while we were all asleep. Also awaiting us was the assortment of cold meats, fresh fruit, and other breakfast fare.

Earlier, I had glanced out of my window to check where we were and found that we were moving very quickly with the steely-grey waters of the Nile speeding past. As yet, everything looked quiet outside, but the sun had already cast its glow across the fields, where the inhabitants of the little hamlets beyond had already begun their work for the day.

During the early hours, we had left our mooring where we had been tied up for security reasons with other cruise boats for the night, and had sailed another thirty odd miles south to reach our destination at Edfu. There, we were to experience another splendid excursion into Egypt's past by visiting the temple dedicated to Horus, whose image as a falcon we had seen many times at Luxor and Karnak. According to mythology, Horus, depicted as a falcon-headed man, was the sky-god of the Nile Valley whose eyes were the sun and the moon. He was also the son of Osiris and Isis after she had magically made herself pregnant with Osiris after assembling all his body parts together, and it was at Edfu that Horus avenged the murder of his father by defeating his uncle Seth in a fierce battle, after which the gods proclaimed him ruler of Egypt. Seth was banished back to the wilderness and became the voice of thunder. Thereafter, Edfu became a shrine to Horus to which loyal worshippers made their pilgrimage to celebrate this triumph of good over evil. They also assembled at Edfu to celebrate the union of Horus with his consort Hathor whose statue was brought from Dendera annually to spend one night alone with him in the temple.

When we reached the little town of Edfu on the western bank of the Nile, we were greeted by the splendid sight of the temple's massive twin pylons rising 36m (108ft) high and extending over 70m (210ft) across, making them the largest structures to be found outside Karnak.

The Ptolemaic kings who succeeded the pharaohs, continued to preserve the ancient cults and constructed temples to the same design as those of previous times. The one at Edfu was begun during the reign of Ptolemy III in 237 BC, but construction continued for another two hundred years until the reign of Ptolemy XII (80-52 BC) the father of Cleopatra, also known as Neos Dionysus. It was said that the lavish decorations alone took a hundred years to complete.

The temple was discovered by a visiting French expedition in 1798 who found it had been almost completely buried under the desert sand, which had helped to preserve it. Only its upper columns and pylons were visible, and like Esna, the populace had also built their homes on its roof tops. It was not until the 1960s when Frenchman Auguste Mariette, who was director of *Les Services des Antiques Egyptiennes* began removing the mud huts and the mountains of rubbish accumulated by the inhabitants, did the entire temple revealed itself with its roof intact. A painting produced by the Scottish artist David Roberts at the time recorded the mountains of sand piled up against the structure and almost reaching the top of the forecourt's columns. He was also able to record for posterity the original colours which had miraculously survived.

One of the many wonderful discoveries made at the temple was the written account in hieroglyphics of the temple's construction during its many phases recalled by an unknown priest of the first century who had witnessed the proceedings and may also had taken part in them. This amazing account was inscribed on a single panel that stretched some 300m around the lower part of the outer enclosure wall for everyone to see. The priest even mentioned the day Ptolemy III, Euergetes I (246-222 BC), lay the measuring rope for the foundations, stating that it was on the "7th day of the month of Epiphi" which corresponded with 23rd August 237 BC, during the tenth year of Ptolemy's reign. The priest also recorded that it also took place on the sixth day of the Festival of Senut, a date on which foundations for a new temple were usually laid. And, amid poetic language

The Inner Courtyard

honouring Horus and other gods he called Horus "the god of the Dappled Plumage", "His Majesty in Edfu" and "Lord of the Heaven". The priest recorded that the Shrine of the Divine Winged Disc (Naos) was completed during the third month of Shemu (3rd February 176 BC) in the time of Ptolemy IV, Philopator (222-205 BC) after a total of twenty-five years. This was followed by decorating the walls with reliefs and hanging doors to the chambers which were completed in the sixteenth year of Ptolemy IV's reign. But when a rebellion in the south broke out (no details given) work on the temple was temporarily suspended and was only resumed when Ptolemy V succeeded to the throne in 205 BC and put an end to the troubles.

The work of installing the double doors to the chapels and erecting the main gate of Great Victory was said to have commenced on the first day of the month of Shef-bedet (3rd February 176 BC) under Ptolemy VI, named as "Heir to Epiphanes". The doors were made of conifer wood and then covered with bronze. And during his reign the work was resumed on the Naos which included the tracing of the inscriptions in ink, the embellishment of its walls in gold, and the gilding of its doors which was completed by the eighteenth day of the fourth month of the Shemu season during the reign of Ptolemy VIII, and said to have been on 10th September 142 BC. There was no mention of Ptolemy VII, but Ptolemy VIII, also named as Heir of Epiphanes, was said to have completed the work, the whole proceedings having taken ninety-five years since the laying of the measuring rope. The measurements of the Naos were given as 105 cubits long, 63 cubits wide, and over 22 cubits high. A cubit was an ancient form of measurement, and one cubit measured the length of a man's forearm. When the Naos had been completed, the priest recorded that there was great rejoicing when this part of the temple was formerly handed over to its owner "Horus of Behdety, the Great God and Lord of Heaven".

The celebrations for this momentous event began early in the morning as people from Dendera also joined in the festivities with an abundance of food including fat geese for burnt offerings and vast quantities of myrrh, the smoke of which was said to have blotted out the sky. It was said that drunkenness was also rife and people danced with garlands around their necks. The occasion was highlighted by the presence of the Falcon Horus who was paraded in front of the crowds in his processional boat.

Then, during the ninth day of the season of Shemu, (2nd July 140 BC) the measuring rope for the foundation of the Pronaos (Outer Hypostyle Hall) was laid, and its completion was recorded as being on the 5th September 124 BC. This too was celebrated with drunkenness and great merriment when it was ceremoniously handed over to Horus.

Following the completion of the Pronaos, foundations for the enclosure wall, the courtyard and the pylons were made, and it was during this phase that Ptolemy VIII died on the 28th June 116 BC. The unknown priest also went on to give the measurements of the enclosure wall as 240 cubits long, 90 cubits wide, and 20 cubits high, and each of the two pylon towers measured 60 cubits high and 120 cubits long, and 21 cubits wide.

The 300m (900ft) long history continued to give precise details of every room in the temple with their individual measurements, and it is from this valuable account that archaeologists have learned so much about the temple and its long construction which finally ended during the reign of Ptolemy XII on the 5th December 57 BC. The priest also named all those Ptolemaic kings who had contributed to the temple, and added that their cartouches were 'written' inside the temple as a recognition of their services. And, it was by no means a bold boast when he stated that 'the temple would endure forever'.

The translation of this unique inscription was first made in 1932 by Emile Chassinat, but a more reliable version was said to have been made in 1961 by Constant de Wit, and appeared in a publication by Dieter Kurth, Professor of Archaeology at the University of Hamburg which appeared on sale at the site.

Records also revealed that the nineteenth century archaeologists had a difficult time in clearing away the sand and cleaning out the temple of the rubbish dropped through its roof by those who had lived there. The squatters had also used the temple as places of work, whose fires had contributed to the pollution of its interior. And much to the archaeologists' disgust, the temple had also been used as a communal lavatory. Once the temple had been finally cleared of its rubbish, scholars began to arrive to document its precious inscriptions. But with no suitable accommodation available, they made use of some of the temple's rooms for storing equipment and as living quarters, using floor mats on which to sleep as a protection against the scorpions which also sought refuge there.

Initially the work of recording the precious texts proved difficult, as without the benefit of electricity, they complained that the light was inadequate, and had to resort to using petroleum lamps which gave off a foul smelling fog that made matters worse. Ladders were essential to reach the top of the columns, but as the light there was very poor, one scholar complained that the opera glasses he was using were causing him considerable eye strain! Of course, they did not have the luxury of electricity at the time, neither did they have the advantage of modern day technology such as computers and digital cameras which play an important role in present-day recording and exploration.

Edfu: The Façade of the Pylon showing Horus with Hathor looking at the King smitting his enemies

However, our particular study of the temple started with the spectacle of the pylons with their twin towers hovering above us, and each one containing a massive carving of Ptolemy XII, wearing the double crown and slaying his enemies, with the figures of Horus and Hathor standing by approvingly. Above the group were a line of figures representing other gods sitting in a neat row. The pylons, standing 75m (115ft) high and extending 137m (260ft) across, provided a stunning entrance with the stone gleaming rosy-pink in the bright morning sunshine.

In between the pylons was a lintel above the central doorway which had created a narrow shelf, and it was there that priests put a living falcon to represent Horus during the festivals. Also a live falcon was taken from the sacred aviary and 'crowned' in the courtyard at a ceremony called the *Festival of Coronation*, after which it was taken to a dark chamber where it 'reigned' for a year as the symbol of the living king. This ritual eventually initiated the School for Falconry that was established at Edfu.

Once through the doorway, we entered a large rectangular courtyard which was surrounded on three sides by a splendid colonnade of thirty tall columns with lavishly decorated capitals, and was the most beautiful part of the temple. It was hard to believe that the court had once been deeply covered in sand. But the main attraction there were the reliefs on the inner wall of the left pylon portraying the festivals with a scene of the *Feast of the Beautiful Meeting* showing Horus towing Hathor's barge to the temple, and the concluding ritual when both were taken to the Sanctuary to be locked in together for the night. The wall of the other pylon had scenes showing the pair emerging from the temple and Hathor's departure to Dendera. Without knowing it, those who had created these images had provided the future with a living record of these extraordinary events and explained the religious myths that featured so prominently in the Egyptians' everyday lives. The discovery of an ancient papyrus also provided an excellent record of the festivities. Translated, it read:

"Wine flows in the districts… Myrrh is on the fire and can be smelt a mile away. The priests and officiants are dressed in fine linen, and the king's party is made fine in its regalia. Its young people are drunk, its populace is happy, its young girls are beautiful to see. Jollity is all around it. Carnival is in all its districts, and there is no sleep until dawn."

From this description, it appears that nothing has changed throughout the centuries. It could fit any celebrations taking place today.

The Majestic figure of Horus as a Hawk
The panel behind shows Ptolemy making offereing to the god Horus

The Courtyard also presented some interesting reliefs on the screens in between the columns. The one on the right showed Ptolemy IX making offerings to Horus, Hathor, and their son Ihy. And on the opposite side, his successor, Ptolemy X, was making his own offerings to the trio. But dominating the top end of the courtyard and standing to the left of the entrance in to the Main Hall was the majestic looking statue of Horus as a falcon in black granite, standing over 3m (9ft) high and wearing the double crown of Egypt. Most noticeable was the defiant gaze of the large transfixed eyes that appeared to offer no welcome. This remarkable sculpture was regarded as being the most magnificent carving of the falcon-god.

Once inside the Hypostyle Hall, we found ourselves surrounded by a cluster of columns that reached the ceiling. Arranged in rows of three on either side of the walkway, we found their shadows refreshingly cool, providing us with a pleasing respite from the rising heat of the morning sun. The layout was similar to the temple at Esna, but here there were two rooms to explore: The one to the left was the Chamber of Consecrations where the king or high priest dressed for the rituals, and the one on the right was the Library, where all the sacred texts had been kept. Inside, there was an interesting relief of Seshat, the goddess of writing. Although the rooms were empty, their decorations gave an indication of their importance at the celebrations.

Next, was the Festival Hall, the oldest part of the temple which had been built during the reign of Ptolemy III (246-227 BC), but was completed by his son. And, as we progressed further into the temple, the rooms became smaller and darker, with only the occasional floor lights to reflect light upwards, or an occasional ceiling light to guide us through. In many instances, a torch would have been desirable to highlight some of the scenes, but more importantly, we wished we could have deciphered the hieroglyphs telling all the stories. This second hall had twelve columns supporting the ceiling in orderly rows of two, and its walls had scenes of the pharaoh worshipping both Horus and Hathor. The Festival Hall also contained three of the chambers crucial to the ceremonies. The chamber in the top left hand corner had been the Laboratory where the perfumes and incense had been prepared. There too, like at Dendera, the scribes had preserved their recipes by displaying them around the walls. In the other two chambers, offerings such as wine and other liquids had been prepared in the one, and solid offerings such as fruit and meat had been stored and prepared in the other before taking them into the Hall of Offerings next door.

Daily worship at the temple took the form of three services. In the morning the priests presented the offerings of food in the presence of the Horus' statue, and at midday there were offerings of purification with incense. In the evening, there was also the ritual where purification was carried out.

To the left and right of this narrow chamber were two circular staircases, one on either side, again as at Dendera, up which the priests had carried the statues of Horus and Hathor to the roof to be rejuvenated by the morning sun at New Year. Their walls had also been vividly inscribed with processional scenes.

Beyond the Hall of Offerings was the Sanctuary of Horus, the holy of holies where the gold covered statue of Horus was kept. The Sanctuary was in its own enclosed room and occupied a central position in the temple. It was also the darkest with the only light coming in through three small openings in the ceiling. However, it was sufficient for us to see the black granite shrine in its centre and the table on which the offerings had been laid. The most significant scenes on the lower part of the wall were those of the pharaoh entering the Sanctuary and worshipping Horus and Hathor who were in the presence of their deified parents, Osiris and Isis.

The Sanctuary was surrounded on three sides by smaller chambers, one of which had contained the life size replica of Horus' ceremonial barge. This replica had been made by Auguste Mariette, after the original had been taken away to the British Museum where it was put on display.

To the right of the Sanctuary was the New Year Chapel through which the statues went on their journey to the roof. It was worth visiting as there was a beautiful blue-coloured relief of the goddess Nut stretched across its ceiling. The steps leading up to the chapel had severely worn down and appeared lopsided. They were certainly not safe to mount, and as the ceiling relief was similar to the one at Dendera, there was no need to.

We made our exit through the west door of the first Hypostyle Hall, and found ourselves in an alleyway situated between the temple and its outer protective walls. There, we were able to study at leisure the complex figures and hieroglyphic symbols that filled the outer west walls of the temple, and more than ever felt at a disadvantage in not being able to decipher the symbols which the ancient scribes had so meticulously carved. It was incredible to see all the recurring symbols and figures measuring the same size all along the wall to the exact millimetre. This accomplishment was a credit to the

Workers preparing a hoist to reinstate a second statue of Horus

patience and great skill of the artists involved, the like of which the world has not seen again.

Meanwhile, on the other side of the temple, the east wall told the story of the combat between Horus and Seth, with Seth portrayed as a hippopotamus which grew smaller and smaller as the story went along until, finally, he was transformed into a tiny piece of cake and eliminated when the priests devoured him.

At the top right-hand side of the alley, we came across a flight of steps which led steeply downwards into a narrow tunnel that formed the Nilometer. This was one of the unique warning devices to register the level of the river during its annual flooding. Where the tunnel curved to the left, there were signs that the river had actually entered at some time in the past and had left tell-tail watermarks on its walls. In any event, the Roman builders had ensured that the temple had been built on higher ground to prevent flooding. The outer protective walls had a similar function, but they had not bargained that in the coming centuries the temple would be abandoned as a place of worship, and that the advancing desert would take possession.

Before leaving the temple, the smart looking colonnaded Mammisi to the right of the entrance was also worth a visit. There, the divine birth of Horus was celebrated, and his incarnation as a reigning monarch was performed each year at the *Coronation Festival*. Inside were scenes of Isis suckling Horus as a baby and then a young man.

The outside compound had a cafeteria and a tourist bazaar where young men in flowing white robes tried to entice us into buying their colourful wares. The richly embroidered garments looked inviting, but resisting the temptation, and the vendors' persistent calls for attention, we moved on, and wondered what else we would see at our next destination.

KOM OMBO: THE TEMPLE OF HAROERIS AND SOBEK

Each morning we were greeted with a different scene as our boat made its leisurely journey southwards and, after Edfu, the scenery began to change quite dramatically. As, whilst the desert encroached ever near on the west bank, the craggy mountains on the eastern side also grew nearer to the river, and in one place, the main road which had followed us southwards, was quite visible as it wound its way through the ridge of mountains. Beyond the strip of cultivated fields along the eastern bank, the main railway line from Cairo had also followed us southwards, to pass Kom Ombo on its way to Aswan, as indeed were we.

Kom Ombo was situated on a bend in the Nile, thirty-four miles south of Edfu, and was where the harvested sugar cane in this area was taken by train loads to the sugar refinery located alongside the river bank. As well as this thriving industry, Kom Ombo was noted for building feluccas in its boat yards, also located on the river.

In ancient times, Kom Ombo was known as Pa-Sobek – Land of Sobek, the crocodile god. It had also been on the caravan route to Nubia from where slaves, exotic goods and more importantly gold from its mines were brought into Egypt. The Ptolemaic kings had also made it a military centre for training elephants for warfare as a counter measure against their rivals and neighbours, the Seleucids, who were using Indian elephants.

But its greatest attraction was undoubtedly the imposing Temple of Haroeris and Sobek standing proudly above the eastern bank of the Nile, with its colonnaded façade welcoming us in the afternoon sunshine. Excitedly, we followed the curving footpath that led us through the ruined Gateway of Neos Dionysus and past the little Chapel of Hathor where some mummified crocodiles from an adjacent crocodile cemetery had been found in the 1970s and put on display. As it was overcrowded with sightseers and the mummies indistinguishable in the darkness, we moved on.

Kom Ombo: Approaches to the Temple of Sobek and Haroeris

The Temple's Riverside Façade

However, that was not the case as we entered the Outer Hypostyle Hall with its colonnaded façade. With the sunlight flooding its interior, appreciation of its columns and carvings was made all the more enjoyable.

Overall, the temple was another brilliant example of Greco-Roman architecture, with the Ptolemaic kings again retaining the old traditional methods of temple building. It was smaller than either Dendera or Edfu, and had a dual layout, having been split down the middle, with one side for the worship of Haroeris (Horus the Elder), and the other mirroring its neighbour for the worship of Sobek. The temple also had two separate entrances, above which was the insignia of the winged sun-disc and the cobra. It was built under Ptolemy VII (145-116 BC), and was extended by Ptolemy IX who erected the pylon. In later years, the Roman Emperor, Trajan (AD 14), added his own contribution by creating the forecourt. The siting of the temple so close to the river had disastrous results when, over time, the Nile had washed away its pylons and part of Trajan's forecourt. However, most of the temple's walls had remained intact, although some of its interior ones had vanished, as had the roof which allowed the sunlight to penetrate through.

The columns of the Outer Hypostyle Hall were richly decorated with floral capitals showing the heraldic lily of Upper Egypt and a papyrus, symbol of the Delta, carved around their bases. One relief of note showed Ptolemy XII at his coronation in the presence of Haroeris, Sobek and two goddesses: Nekhbet, the vulture goddess, and Wadjet, the snake goddess, whose roles were to protect the pharaoh. There was also one featuring Ptolemy making offerings to the same deities at the back of the hall where the architraves balancing at the top of the pillars were decorated with flying vultures. The most pleasing feature was that they had still retained their original colours of red and blue which brought them more to life.

The open Inner Hypostyle Hall was just as revealing in that it had the image of Sobek as a crocodile between the doorways with grand reliefs of Ptolemy II making offerings to the gods around the shafts of the pillars.

Beyond, were the vestibules, with each one a step higher than the other, and their decoration was attributed to Ptolemy VI (around AD 180), among which were scenes showing the foundation of the temple with Seshat, the goddess of writing, measuring the dimensions. The right-sided half of the temple dedicated to Sobek had texts dedicated to him and curiously, there was a small relief of a woman giving birth on the southern wall. The architraves suspended across the pillars there were again decorated with flying vultures, and their original colours still intact.

The two Sanctuaries had no surviving walls dividing them, and were open to the elements. They lay practically side by side within a few metres of each other, but their individual altars of free standing blocks of granite had been deliberately smashed. Originally, there had been a secret corridor between the two from where the priests, having entered via an underground crypt, would 'speak' to the gods. The daily offerings to Haroeris and Sobek in the Hall of Offerings were to keep the temple in a state of purity, and only the priests were allowed inside to conduct the rituals.

The outside walls also produced some interesting aspects of the temple. Bas reliefs there showed Ptolemy XII being purified by the gods Thoth and Horus, with another scene showing the monarch in the presence of Sobek.

The back wall also produced an interesting array of surgical instruments which included scalpels, bone saws and some deadly looking knives, all of which were said to be similar to the instruments used by present-day surgeons, but were probably used for slaughtering animals for sacrifices there. There had also been a colossal relief on the outside western wall showing Ptolemy with his enemies at his feet and a majestic looking lion at his side, but only the feet of the monarch could be seen and those of his foes. And, judging by the size of the feet, this relief had probably reached the entire height of the wall. Another surprise around the corner was the row of stone coffins with their maker's chisel marks still visible. Our guide told us, that the temple had also offered the rich people of the district a-made-to- measure coffin service.

The gravelled courtyard also produced some other items of interest with the remains of a small Mammisi in which were scenes of Ptolemy VIII seated in a boat before the god Min who was famed for his strength and was responsible for the fertility of all animals and humans. Nearby was a deep well with numbered steps that had measured the depth of the Nile when it was in flood, and was used to charge local farmers according to the number the water had reached. Nearby, was a square enclosure where crocodiles were said to have been reared. Water for this shallow pool had been piped directly from the Nile. In ancient times, crocodiles were kept as pets and mummified upon death, and special cemeteries were created for their burial, such as the one found during recent excavations. Their mummified forms were also given as offerings to the gods. It was at Kom Ombo, just below the temple, that crocodiles were seen to bask on the river bank.

The King making offerings to Sobek

Surviving portion of Colossal Relief

The Nile at Aswan

There was a pleasant view of the river in both directions from the retaining wall at the end of the forecourt, as feluccas with their triangular white sails made their way northwards, creating one of those never-to-be-forgotten images of the day.

A few years later, the approach to the temple was changed so that people came from the direction of the town, and where steps had previously led up from the Nile, a smart tea garden had opened with straw canopies offering shade over the individual tables. And, by 2010, horse-drawn carriages were able to drop visitors close to the ruin of the first pylon, as indeed could all vehicles. This solitary ruin was a prominent landmark, and guided people to the staircase that ultimately led up to the temple's forecourt. On reflection, though, the old curving pathway had provided a much easier access to the temple, nevertheless the newly built terrace at the top of the stairs had provided an excellent platform from which to admire the surrounding views.

Our visit to Kom Ombo had practically marked the end of the cruise. All that remained was to sail southwards to Aswan, Egypt's most southern city where, for all cruise boats, it was the 'end of the line'. There, the High Dam had cut off the Nile and made further navigation south impossible. Beyond lay the newly created Lake Nasser that had submerged the whole of Nubia, and stretched 300 miles southwards, almost reaching the Sudanese border.

This last stretch of the Nile was still full of wonder as we watched flocks of egrets wading amongst the reeds and rising up like a mighty cloud when they flew off to another spot. We could see their white plumage in the distance long before we came across them. We could also see the minarets of distant mosques telling us that we were nearing Aswan.

Although Aswan was our furthermost point on board *The Nile Commodore*, there were still some surprises left in store.

AGILKIA ISLAND: TEMPLES OF ISIS

Every day had presented some kind of surprise which had turned out to be an amazing experience, and today was no exception when we were driven to Shallal dock where a flotilla of motorboats were waiting to take us over to Agilkia Island. There, the Temples of Isis had been relocated to prevent them from being lost forever under the Nile, following the completion of the High Dam.

Originally the temple complex had been situated on Philae Island which, with Agilkia was part of a small group of islands situated south of the Aswan Dam. Philae had already been submerged for six months of the year following the construction of the dam, so it was imperative that the temples should be transported stone by stone to higher ground and saved for posterity. This remarkable operation took place during the years 1972 – 1980 after UNESCO had called upon the world to save the Nubian temples, Abu Simbel among them, and the individual temples were finally relocated on Agilkia Island in the same places they had occupied on Philae. The island was then landscaped to match their original surroundings. It was a feat of human endeavour and expertise.

The temples had been the scene of pilgrimage since Ptolemaic times when Isis became a popular deity with the Romans and her cult flourished throughout the Roman Empire as she was venerated along with their goddess Venus. The temples were the largest to be devoted to Isis and, apart from the small structure built by the 30th Dynasty pharaoh Nectabebo I around the fourth century BC, the rest of the complex was built over the next 500 years by the Ptolemies and succeeding Roman Emperors, up until the fifth century AD when the last of the hieroglyphs were said to have ended around AD 437.

But many of them had been understandably defaced by occupying Christians, and later by invading Muslims. Numbering fifteen in all, the Temples' walls expressed many religious beliefs, and as such, historians have considered them to be the richest library recording the religious history of Ancient Egypt.

Agilkia Island: Approaching the temple

The boats at Shallal waiting to take us to the island

The worship of Isis at Philae was said to have begun around 550 BC, after which the island became a popular resort and a place of exploration during the Roman era. But, in AD 550, the Emperor Justinian closed the temples and transformed it into a centre for Christianity, whereupon the Christians left their mark by carving crosses inside the main temple.

Travelling Europeans "rediscovered" it in the nineteenth century, after which the Temples became a popular destination, even though, during those times when the island was flooded, they could only view the submerged structures from a boat. However, due to the expertise of modern technology, modern-day visitors have the benefit of walking through the temple complex and seeing it in all its former glory. On skimming across deep blue waters to reach the island in our motor boat, we headed around the southern headland to see the graceful columns of Trajan's "kiosk" rising up behind the trees at the top of the cliff, creating a romantic picture.

The 'Kiosk' of Trajan

Temple of Isis: Agilika Island saved from Philea
The Temple pf Nectanebo I

Isis with her son Horus and Hathor on the main temple's pylon

The columns of the Great West Colonnade

The Pylons at the far end of the temple

But it was the graceful structure of Nectabebo I which delighted us upon arriving at the enormous open space of the Outer Temple Court with its long colonnade on either side. It was the oldest structure in the complex, and built by him in honour of his "mother Isis". The double capitals of the remaining columns had the traditional flower-shape with the head of Hathor supporting the architraves above them. The layout of these columns made a compact little square enclosure and, it was thought, that the Romans had copied this unique design with building structures they called "Kiosks". The screen walls, however, carried the unusual design of Ureaus serpents that had been used for Zoser's complex at Saqqara, nearly three thousand years earlier.

Beyond the Vestibule, the colonnades made another impressive scene, but the ones on the western side were in a better state of preservation and had finely carved capitals. They also marked the outer boundary of the Island which stretched in one long straight line. The columns on the opposite side had been left undecorated, nevertheless they made a striking pathway to the main temple. At one time, the Temple of Arensnupis, worshipped as the "Good Companion of Isis", had abutted the eastern colonnade, but only its foundations had survived, as had the ruins of the Chapel of Mandulis, a Nubian god of nearby Kalabsha. At the head of the eastern colonnade lay the ruined Temple of Imhotep, the architect of Zoser's Step Pyramid at Saqqara, and who was later deified as a god of healing. Its walls showed Ptolemy IV in the presence of several gods including Khnum, Isis and Osiris, paying homage. There had even been a Temple devoted to the worship of Hathor. Its ruins lay to the east of the main Temple with only two of its Hathor-headed columns in situ. Its most interesting reliefs were those of musicians with the god of childbirth, Bes playing a harp.

There was also a Mammisi, built by Ptolemy IV (222-205 BC) in honour of Horus' birth, and in which he attended the birthday rituals. And, as is to be expected, the façade's columns had the head of Hathor above each one. However, its Sanctuary's walls contained some lovely scenes of Hathor suckling a child that represented the young Ptolemy, but these had been badly defaced. In later years, the Emperor Augustus (30BC – AD 14) also made a contribution by adding some reliefs of his own.

But the most commanding structure of the forecourt was the enormous pylon at its far end which marked the entrance into the temple itself, and whose walls portrayed an enormous figure of Ptolemy XII smiting his enemies in true pharaonic fashion with Hathor and Horus looking on. A small ramp led us through into the great space of the Hypostyle Hall where its two rows of columns and walls had been left unpainted by its builder, Ptolemy VII Euergetes II, although there were scenes of him making sacrifices to the gods on the undecorated columns. However, when the Emperor Justinian put an end to the Isis cult and the temple was no longer available to worship her, the Copts turned the temple into a church and even erected a granite altar there which had been carved with the Coptic cross.

The temple had also contained an Inner Sanctuary where the goddess' gold statue had been kept inside a red granite shrine which had been carved on the orders of Ptolemy VIII Euergetes (170-116 BC). This beautiful shrine was transported to London for display at the British Museum, but the stone base on which the goddesses' sacred barque had stood was still in place. Interestingly, it had been inscribed with the names of Ptolemy III (246-221 BC), and his wife Berenice. Then a surprise was a Shrine to Osiris, situated on the roof where the artists had portrayed the entire myth in revealing scenes, showing Isis gathering up Osiris' dismembered body, and the gods assembling it for its solar rebirth. It was then borne away to a papyrus swamp by the four sons of Horus, to be anointed with holy water attended by Anubis. At the time of the visit, the roof was out of bounds.

Back outside in the bright sunshine, the Kiosk of Trajan standing on the eastern side of the island and overlooking the Nile, glowed with a radiance that appeared to separate it from the other structures, and its classical design identified it as being of Roman origin. It was said to have been unfinished, probably because it had no roof, and had been given the name "The Pharaoh's Bed". Its elegance certainly earned it as being the most popular structure on the Island. Inside the "kiosk" there were no rooms, but its internal walls contained some very large reliefs honouring the various deities, and being open to the sunshine, they were very clear to see.

The Gate of Diocletan was another attractive structure close to the cliff tops on that side of the island, and also looked very Roman in character. It was named after the Emperor Diocletan (AD 284-305) and was probably built during his reign, making it the last to have been built there. It had also been completely submerged by the Nile whilst on Philae, but during the recovery operation, it was safely brought to the surface, stone by stone, by a team of British divers from the Royal Navy, and then transported to its

The Gateway of Diolectan

present location. On looking at it, like the others, one would have thought that it had always been there.

Close by was another Roman structure – the Temple of Augustus, – named after the Roman Emperor, but very little of it had remained. It was amazing to think that even its pathetic ruins had been transported there in the same position they had occupied on Philae. Had we not known that fact, we could have been standing on Philae itself.

On exploring the far end of the island, another large part of the temple came to light when, beyond another pylon on the other side of the Hypostyle Hall, there was another extensive courtyard flanked by columns and as large as the front one, making this temple almost as long as the island itself.

These were the enduring images we left behind on saying farewell to the island, and after being 'skimmed' back to Shallal, we were taken back to the refreshing coolness of *The Nile Commodore* where it was to moor at Aswan for the next two days. There, an appetising buffet awaited us, and once inside, we considered ourselves fortunate to have escaped the increasing temperatures outside. We thought of those we had left queuing to be ferried across to Agilkia. They would be finding exploration of the island at that time of day less comfortable without the benefit of shade.

In our search for the coolest place on board, the shady awnings on the top deck appeared to be the most desirable. In any case, we would already be in the right place when the gong went for tea. And whilst everyone relaxed throughout the afternoon and reflected on the morning's events, it was also a time for recharging one's batteries for the nightly party in the Salon, when the whole deck would reverberate to the sound of laughter and dancing feet.

And, even though we were departing very early the next morning on our optional excursions, we still intended to have some fun. From a choice of visiting Kitchener's Island, or having a flight in a hot air balloon over Aswan, I was in the group heading for the temples of Abu Simbel. And again, the morning could not come soon enough

THE TEMPLES OF RAMSES II AND HIS QUEEN NEFERTARI AT ABU SIMBEL

1. THEIR REMOVAL TO THEIR PRESENT POSITION

These magnificent temples had once been in great danger of being flooded when the 340 mile long Lake Nasser was created after the construction of the Aswan Dam which had been built to provide Egypt with hydro-electric power and secure a sufficient water supply to sustain the country as the Nile itself had done millennia before.

Already the lake had submerged forty-five Nubian villages, and since these temples would also disappear beneath the waters of the newly created lake, the Egyptian Government made a plea to the United Nations in April 1959, for help to save them for posterity. Fifty-one nations rallied to the call, and contributions towards the cost of salvaging them rolled in. Many nations made their own suggestions for preserving them which included the building of a dam to keep the waters at bay, but the Italians went further to suggest that the mountain be cut away and the temples encased in huge concrete boxes reinforced with steel, under which 650 synchronised jacks supported by concrete pillars would raise them little by little until they were clear of the waterline. Another ingenious scheme was also to build a dam, but to allow the temples to be flooded so they could be viewed through reinforced glass similar to an aquarium with a lift to take visitors down from the surface. This was by far the most audacious scheme, but the one presented by Swedish engineers won the day whereby the temples would be cut up into transportable pieces and re-assembled on higher ground. This also appeared to be an ambitious plan but was fraught with danger, as it was feared the sandstone would be far too brittle for cutting and that the precious statues would crumble. But after the engineers had ensured their calculations on the rock stresses were correct, the Swedish scheme was adopted. However, it was not only the great façades that presented a problem. As Ramses had built the temples deep inside the mountain, the task of removing their chambers complete with their walls and ceilings had also to be considered. This was the task presented to UNESCO, and as thirty-six million US dollars had been raised towards the cost of this momentous task, work began in 1964, starting with an immense covering of sand over the façades to protect them whilst the surrounding rock was being cut away. And after this had been completed, iron scaffolding was used to support the ceilings of the inner chambers.

During the four years the work took to complete, 1,041 blocks, each weighing an average of 30 tons, had been individually hand sawn and carefully removed by cranes and numbered for reassembling. A further 1,112 blocks had been cut from the rock around the temples and 33 tons of resin used to consolidate the rock structure. In the case of the giant heads of Ramses, each face was carefully sliced away and hauled to safety by the cranes. They were then covered with sand for protection until they could be reunited with the rest of the statues. This also applied to the heads of the Osiride figures of Ramses inside the temple.

When the temples and all their statuary had been safely removed, it was then the task of recreating the mountain and building it in its new position 90m (270ft) higher up. For this task, two enormous domes of reinforced concrete, supported with steel frames, were built to house each of the temples, and were covered with an estimated 600,000 sq.m of sand and rubble to make them look like as though they were still inside their own individual mountain. The dome over Ramses' temple was positioned at the same angle as before to face directly east, so that the first rays of the rising sun on the 22nd February and 22nd October, the days he celebrated his birthday and Coronation, would highlight his image in the Inner Sanctum, at precisely the same time as it had centuries before. And amazingly, this enormous feat had been achieved with only a day's difference.

The work of moving the two temples was the most incredible feat of dismantling and reconstruction ever attempted by the engineers which had also required an enormous work force. The entire operation had cost forty-two million US dollars, half of which was paid by UNESCO and was completed on the 22nd September 1968, just in time before the lake flooded the enormous caverns which had been left behind by the excavations below. Since that date, the old locations have been lying well under the waters of the lake.

Seeing the temples safely in their picturesque setting beside the shores of Lake Nasser has stirred many a heart. Even Ramses would have approved that such care and precision had been taken to get them there safely.

The slicing up of Ramses during the evacuation to higher ground

2. THE VISIT

To see these magnificent structures was the highlight of the entire cruise, and one I had long dreamed of making, but as it was situated beyond Aswan, we had no option but to fly south down the entire length of Lake Nasser to Abu Simbel's very own airport.

Considering that Aswan was not on any major air route, it was surprising to discover its terminal building had a palatial interior of grey marble that would have befitted any royal palace. The marble floors shone like glass, and were so reflective, it was as though they were covered with water. The walls and pillars also shone like glass and created a cooling and relaxing place whilst we waited our departure which was delayed. It was a luxury not afforded to travellers at other airports, and it was not so busy either at that time of morning with no people milling around crowded shops, and queues waiting at the checking-in desk. And surprisingly, there was no sound of departing planes either as one would have expected at such a generously proportioned and lavishly built terminal.

Once on board our small *Egypt Air* aeroplane, seating just two passengers aside, two military jets screamed down the runway adjacent to us and shot into the blue in a matter of seconds. As Aswan airport had also served as a military airbase used by the Egyptian Air Force, we gathered that it was probably the pending departure of the military jets that had delayed our own.

The half an hour 350 mile long flight to Abu Simbel airport was certainly unusual. For such a small aircraft, we did not expect the services of a stewardess, but soon after take-off, we were given a carton of fruit juice and a small packet of biscuits by a courteous young man in uniform who might have been part of the crew on the flight deck. But it was the stunning views of Lake Nasser that caught everyone's attention. From the air it looked like an inland sea, with its curling shores creating hundreds of tiny inlets that had become the habitat of crocodiles, an abundance of fish, and many species of birds. The colour of the golden-brown headlands meeting bright blue waters provided a unforgettable picture during the flight south.

We lost no time passing through the small airport at Abu Simbel which had been in operation long before the temples were moved when there had been direct flights to and from Khartoum. Otherwise, travellers would have arrived either by boat, or by travelling across the desert from Wadi Halfa.

Abu Simbel: The Domed Temple of Ramses II

Our transit through the terminal was swift, and our waiting coaches soon transported us the short distance to the famous site. Excitement was in the air as our arrival coincided with others, and anxious to see the temples, we all hurried down the curving road leading directly to the lake. Our pulses quickened as we saw the top of the mountain encasing Ramses' temple. And once we had rounded the corner, the first view facing us was Nefertari's temple, standing at right angles to Ramses' which was facing the lake, as it had done previously at its old site. Both temples looked magnificent standing close to each other, and situated on their own sandy bay facing the lake. It was a magical moment, one to savour and capture the splendour of the sculptures adorning their facades.

But it was Ramses' temple standing 33m (165ft) high and 35m (105ft) wide, that really took one's breath away as the most eye-catching features of its great façade were the three colossi of a seated Ramses wearing the double crown of a united Egypt incorporating the familiar *Uraeus* of the Cobra goddess Wadjyt. There had been four seated pharaohs, but the third one had collapsed after an earthquake soon after the temple had been built, causing the head of Ramses to fall at his feet. There again, the modern engineers had taken the trouble to re-site it exactly where it had fallen. As Ramses was so particular about his monuments, if he had known about the earthquake's damage, he would surely have had another statue made.

Each colossi measured over 20m high and together they dominated the façade with their commanding presence. Certainly, their height had been maximised even more by the tall slabs of stone on which the feet of Ramses rested, and true to form, they were covered with decorative hieroglyphics recording his life and achievements.

Standing beside Ramses' legs were the little statuettes of his offspring: two daughters who were named as Nebttaui and Bentanat, and a son Amun-hir-khepshef. The little figure standing against the third colossus was a son, identified as Prince Ramses. There was also a much larger and beautifully preserved one of Ramses queen, Nefertari, who was actually his daughter whom he married before he became pharaoh. Her name meant "Beautiful Companion". She certainly was that, and was regarded as the favourite of his four wives. She was seen standing next to the third colossi with long plaited hair and wearing the distinctive vulture headdress, the insignia of a queen. On top of this was a crown composed of sacred cobras with a cartouche in the centre. On the opposite side, and next to the fallen colossi, there was a similarly sized statuette of his mother Queen Tuya who was also shown with long braided hair and wearing the vulture headdress. Below the thrones were some falcons to represent the presence of Horus protecting his king.

The reason why Ramses wanted his statues to be so large was to intimidate his Sudanese neighbours across the border, about 16 miles away. But, no matter how intimidating Ramses intended to be, he was portrayed with a kindly face, having a contented expression with the hint of a smile and looking serenely across the waters. The face was said to have been a true portrait of him. Each of these magnificent heads alone measured 4m (12ft) across from ear to ear, with the mouth measuring just over 1m (3ft) wide. Each ear lobe had a small circular depression which suggested that Ramses had worn earrings. His cartouche had also been stamped on each right shoulder as well as appearing above his head. An inscription recording the marriage of Ramses with a Hittite princess, who was given the Egyptian name Matneferurte, was also carved close to the statues. Next to it was a relief showing her father, the Hittite king, Muwatallish, presenting her to Ramses. According to records, the marriage was arranged to consolidate peace between Egypt and the Hittites who had been battling it out ever since Seti I's reign, eventually culminating at the Battle of Qadesh in 1274 BC. This treaty was the first in the history of mankind to have been made between nations to promote peace, and took place on the 28th November, during the thirty-fourth year of Ramses' reign, around 1338 BC, which would have made Ramses about sixty years old. He died in 1237 BC at the age of ninety-two, after being on the throne for sixty-seven years.

On looking at the entire façade, it was difficult to see the joins where it had been cut. Everything looked as though they had always been there, even the row of baboons situated above the statues. They were sacred to Thoth, the God of Wisdom, and their function was to greet each rising sun. Even the buttresses on either side of the temple had been transported to their original positions.

The entrance into the temple was between the great statues, with the sides of the thrones creating a kind of corridor carved with a delightful scene of the Nile god entwining their individual emblems in an act of unity. Below were scenes of captive figures herded together by rope. Above the doorway was the sinister figure of Ra-Horakhty, the falcon-headed god with the sun disc and the cobra above his head, and clasping the key of life in each hand. Alongside the god were images of Ramses making offerings to Maat, his deified self and to Ra-Horakhty. A cartouche bearing Ramses' prenomen Usermaat-Re – "Chosen of Ra" – was also written above the door.

Ramses Temple – Abu Simbel: The procession of captives

Statue of Nefertari

The Osiride figures of Ramses II in the Hypostyle Hall

Ramses II Temple: The Sanctuary with Ptah, Amun, Ramses, Ra-Horakhty

The iconic figure of Ramses giving flight to his enemies

In passing through, it was not difficult to miss the enormous amount of graffiti that nineteenth century travellers had carved on Ramses' legs and on the thigh of Nefertari to record their visit there in the mid 1840s. One had even mentioned that he had come from the Austrian Tyrol. But the earliest must surely have been the one that was written in Greek on the leg of the fallen colossus during the 16th Dynasty around 590 BC to say that the army of King Psammetichus had passed that way. By then, the temple was already over a thousand years old.

The wow factor continued with just one step inside the dim interior of the Hypostyle Hall where an avenue of eight statues of Ramses, standing over 10 feet high, flanked the main aisle, and standing in front of the pillars like a royal guard of honour. All showed Ramses in quiet repose wearing the white domed crown of Upper Egypt and standing with arms crossed holding the crook and flail of kingship in the style of Osiris, indicating that he was half mortal king and half god. He was also wearing a skirt with a jewelled belt around the waist from which hung a tassel. The hieroglyphic carvings on either side of the statues, described Ramses as "the good god. Lord of the Two Lands", and "Ramses beloved of Amun" followed by his distinctive cartouches. We were overawed and felt humbled by their presence, and conscious of the sound our footsteps were making in the stillness, we walked gingerly down their ranks. Above us, the ceiling was decorated with the vultures of the goddess Nekhbet. In their role of protecting the pharaoh, they stretched their blue painted wings across the width of the ceiling. The walls, however, provided a great deal of attention as enormous reliefs showed explicit scenes of Ramses in battle at Qadesh which were masterpieces of ancient carving. The most stunning was the famous and iconic scene of Ramses shooting arrows from his chariot. It was inspirational. This picture had been duplicated hundreds of times, but seeing it in its original form was a great privilege. It recorded every detail of Ramses' triumph, including the overturning of chariots and dying prisoners, all carved with great vigour, even the horses with their feathered headdresses had been given fluidity of movement. After becoming more acquainted with the famous battle, we moved through a short corridor that led to two side rooms where offerings had been stored. There again were stunning wall paintings in delicate colours showing Ramses offering wine and food to Amun, Ra-Horakhty and Ptah. Then flying above them all were the ever protective vultures with wings outstretched. Other picturesque scenes included both Isis and Hathor. In the next room the most commanding picture was of both Ramses and Nefertari in their ceremonial robes standing before the sacred barque of Ra-Horakhty. There, Nefertari was holding up a sistrum in each hand, and amusingly, they both looked remarkably like the old fashioned egg whisks. This particular scene was painted in glowing yellow colours, and its appreciation by viewers millennia later would have pleased its creators.

We then came to the Sacred Sanctuary itself, 60m (180ft) inside the mountain, where Ramses sat against the back wall with Ptah, Amun and Ra-Horakhty the three gods to whom he had dedicated the temple. Ramses, who had considered himself a god, was presented in the same size as the others, and sat in between Amun and Ra-Horakhty. Ptah, sat on the far left against the wall holding a staff, but was missing his head. It was a sombre grey scene, and the stonework of the entire small chamber was in a very bad condition, including the statues which had been stripped of their gold casings way back in antiquity. In front of them was a stone block on which the sacred barque had once rested. It was interesting to note that the illumination of Ramses' figure on those two days of the year by the rising sun, lasted about twenty minutes each time, leaving the other statues only partially lit whilst Ptah, on the other hand, remained in total darkness. It was the Frenchman Jean Champollion who was the first to notice this phenomenon, and it became known as the "miracle of the sun".

Leaving them to their silence, we returned to the bright sunlight and set off towards Queen Nefertari's Temple which had been dedicated to the goddess Hathor.

QUEEN NEFERTARI'S TEMPLE

The temple was much smaller that Ramses', being only 17m (221ft) x 17m (221ft), but it had a delightful façade comprising six statues on either side of the entrance with the figures of Nefertari and Ramses standing 10 feet tall in their own individual niches. The fact that Nefertari's statue was the same size as Ramses, demonstrated the high esteem with which he regarded her, as this was an honour not bestowed on any other consort. Above her crown, Nefertari was shown wearing the headdress of Hathor with the sun disc inside the horns of a cow and topped with two ostrich feathers known as the divine feathers of Amun. On the other hand, whilst Ramses was wearing two of his usual crowns, his figure on the extreme right had been given one to match Nefertari's two feathers with the sun disc. The buttresses separating the figures had been deeply carved with hieroglyphic figures that created their own individual designs to add to those inscribed above the door, and together, they produced the most picturesque façade ever seen at any other temple. Translated, the inscriptions read: "Ramses made this temple in the form of an excavation in the hill as an eternal work in the land of Taserin and nothing like it has been seen before". Once more the royals were joined by knee-high statues of their children standing at their feet with Ramses having four princes, named as Amenhirkhopshef, Pra-hir-unamef, Merire, and Meriatum; whilst Nefertari had seven princesses, two of whom were Meritamun and Henttaui.

Nefertari's own Hypostyle Hall was also a delight with its six pillars, all of which were decorated with the face of Hathor. Beneath were texts which told stories of Ramses and Nefertari. How we wished we could have deciphered them! But the most enchanting were the images of the various gods in all their decorative guises, with Nefertari, robed in a transparent gown and holding a sistrum and flower in each hand. She appeared slim in her transparent robe, and her height was accentuated by her crown of two tall feathers surmounted by the sun disc. Other gods, such as Isis, Mut, Khonsu and Khnum also participated in various scenes, and their decorative guises and apparel turned the Hall into a pleasing colourful display. Ramses also included himself amongst these very feminine scenes by presenting himself as a great warrior and was shown striking an Asian captive with the falcon-headed and crowned Horus in attendance. Nefertari who was also standing to his left in regal robes and wearing the tall feathers, had one arm raised, perhaps as a sign of horror. The scene had not been so well preserved. It was patchy and someone had scrawled some graffiti beside the figure of Horus.

The façade of Nefertari's Temple

The author, pictured at the temples

Nefertari with Ramses and statuets of some of their children

Abu Simbel: The Hypostyle Hall of Nefertari's Temple

Nefertari shown with a sistrum on one of the pillars

Nefertari being crowned by Isis and Hathor
*(Isis wearing the solar disc representing fertility and motherhood instead of her usual
symbol of a throne)*

Off the Hall was the Vestibule where again some delightful scenes filled its walls with one of Nefertari and the young Ramses presenting lotus flowers and a sistrum to a seated Hathor. But the most feminine of all and the most delightful was the picture of Nefertari being crowned by Isis on one side and Hathor on the other. All three were holding the *ankh* and the two goddesses were shown wearing the sun disc surrounded by horns. It had been painted in soft browns and yellows, and was looking as pristine as the day it was created. It was suggested that the predominance of yellow was a reference to Hathor who was also described as "the golden one". The craftsmanship of the carving was such that even in today's art world it would rival any of the recognised masterpieces. To the right of this picture was an equally large one of Ramses presenting wine to the falcon-headed god Ra-Horakhty. At the bottom, the walls had been deeply scarred and someone had scrawled graffiti under Hathor's throne.

At the far end, we had reached 24m (72ft) into the mountain, and the wall there also had a yellowish tinge with a painting of the sacred barque with Hathor holding lotus flowers. There was also a charming relief of Hathor as a cow standing in the barque with Nefertari offering her lilies. Above, flew the familiar images of the sacred vultures guarding the cartouches of Nefertari. On the side walls, Nefertari was shown offering incense to Mut and Hathor, and there was one of Ramses having the last word in paying homage to his queen.

On leaving, we felt that it had been a joy to see such beauty, as without modern means of transport at our disposal, these treasures would not have been within our reach and would have remained completely hidden, as they had been for over three millennia before they came to the world's attention in the nineteenth century.

Following Ramses' death in 1236 BC, it was known that the temples had survived another thousand years until 27 BC when the earthquake had shattered the second colossus. And whilst there was evidence that graffiti had been written on the colossus fifty years later, there had been no further evidence of human activity at the temples, not even to suggest that early Christians had taken over following Nubia's conversion to Christianity, as had occurred on Agilkia Island. Therefore, the two temples passed into obscurity throughout history until 1813, when the Swiss explorer, Louis Burkhardt came across the scene with only the top of Ramses' crowns appearing above the cascade of sand that had completely engulfed the temples. Not knowing what they were, he investigated, and then came across one of Ramses' heads. It must have been a monumental surprise to have discovered something on such a gigantic scale not seen before. The statues had even surpassed the grandeur of the Colossi of Memnon.

Next to arrive on the scene was Giovanni Belzoni in 1817, and after sufficient sand had been removed, he was able to find the entrance and enter. The sand had even infiltrated into Ramses' temple so that a depth of sand was covering the feet of the Osiride figures. David Roberts, the Scottish painter, also visited Abu Simbel twenty-five years after Burkhardt's visit, and recorded for posterity the extraordinary scene of the temple still half buried in sand. Treasure hunters also appeared, but on discovering that there was no treasure to be had, the temples were ignored for a time, and the sand began to creep over the temples once more. However, when all the sand had finally been cleared and the true beauty of the temples were revealed, they were soon put on cruise itineraries at the end of the nineteenth century by Thomas Cook, and became renowned the world over as an important part of Egypt's cultural heritage.

Photography had been prohibited inside both temples, but upon leaving, it was a relief to find a vendor selling pictures of their interiors, thus enabling us to take away records of the images we had seen. And, with those amazing images still in our minds, we reluctantly left for the airport and our return to Aswan. But, even an appetising meal on our return to *The Nile Commodore* could not satisfy the need to complete the day with some kind of event to match our day at Abu Simbel, and true to form, the Salon was put at our disposal for another hilarious round of games and dancing. And, having said goodbye to southern Egypt, we slipped our moorings, and set sail for our leisurely cruise back to where it had all begun at Luxor, happy in the knowledge that, for most of us, we had achieved our wildest dreams and had become more acquainted with the colourful gods and goddesses of ancient Egypt who had opened the doors to their secrets and bygone rituals.

ABOUT THE AUTHOR

Sarah Symons was born in the Swansea valleys, South Wales, but grew up in Shrewsbury. She then moved to Aylesbury where she worked as a medical secretary at Stoke Mandeville Hospital. She continued her secretarial career in London as the BBC and other major companies before she became private secretary to Lord Greenwood and had the privilege of working at the House of Lords.

Sarah eventually returned to Wales and currently lives in Swansea, where she enjoys writing and travelling. She also uses her love for photography to illustrate her books whenever she can.